Red Ribbons

"Coming in second is not all that bad"

Stories from the life of
Reverend
Dr. Robert Geller

written with
Libby James

10/17/08

Thanks
for coming

Bob Geller

Red Ribbons

"Coming in second is not all that bad"

Stories from the life of
Reverend Dr. Robert Geller

written with
Libby James

Published by
The Geller Center for Spritual Development

Printed in the United States of America

Dedication

This book is dedicated to June, who has made a difference in my life since the second Sunday morning in November 1940 when we met; and to our children, Gretchen, Mark, Timothy and Victor.

Acknowledgments

This story is rooted in my relationships and interactions with many people and nature with all its wonders and thousands of forms of life. Community gave me language and most else flows from that source. However, for getting to and into the task of writing, I am deeply indebted to some particular persons. I had good intentions for several years but setting pencil to page may have never made it without the encouragement of and financial support of Bobbie Cook. The editing and final text was ably fleshed out by Libby James who really knows how to turn a phrase, put a story together, and get it published. Much proofing work was done by Tim Geller, Mary Berle and Marianne Rieux.

What's in a title?

In American society, it seems to me that "coming in second" is somehow not enough, whether it be sports, academics, wealth, business, politics or all sorts of contests in the arts. Who remembers the second place people? Aside from distance races in track where I won many firsts in high school and college, I seem to have consistently won a red ribbon for coming in second. All the kudos go to number one. We reserve our hero worship for those who win, not for those who "almost" win. By the time my formal schooling was over, the handwriting was on the wall. And the message had some undeniable advantages.

In Morrill County, Nebraska, in the state-required admission to high school comprehensive examinations, I came in second to a girl. In high school, I was only 16 when I graduated from Dalton High School, so I felt proud to be chosen salutatorian, in other words, number two. My girlfriend at the time beat me out for the top spot.

At Hastings College I graduated second to a woman. In my senior year I was recognized with the coveted Bronco Award for constructive college citizenship, presented to the best all-round student, athlete and individual involved in campus activities. I was mighty proud of that award, the highest honor given by my college. I didn't feel at all diminished by the fact that I shared it with a woman — the first time the award had been given to more than one person. Betty Suehlsen and I were chosen by a faculty-student committee selected by the student body. I came in first that time, but also second.

When I graduated from McCormick Theological Seminary in Chicago, it didn't surprise me that I was to be recognized for having the second-best academic record in my class. In fact, I had a hunch that if my brilliant friend hadn't failed to get all his work in on time, I'd have been number three. There were no women in McCormick at that time, another factor that probably helped me to attain second best. So the title for my story.

Step by Step

Step by step
the longest march can be won,
can be won.
Many stones
Can form an arch, singly none,
singly none,
And by union, what we will, can
be accomplished.
Still, drops of water turn a mill.
singly none
singly none.

From the preamble to the constitution of the United Mine Workers, set to the music of an Irish folk tune.

Contents

Beginnings

"You'd better become a Roman Catholic if you want to be a cop in this town."

I suppose I come by my ecumenical bent quite naturally. The term in Greek means "whole household of God," and is a concept I've embraced for as long as I can remember. I can trace this all-inclusiveness as far back as my great grandfather, Conrad, who came to Boston with his brother, as a young man. When Conrad (always called "Coon") decided he wanted to be a cop, a wise old Bostonian said to him, "You'd better become a Roman Catholic if you want to be a cop in this town."

I found out about this in a rather odd way. In 1986 at a national campus ministers meeting in California I met Rabbi Laura Geller who was director of the Hillel (Jewish) ministry at San Diego State University. She was the first woman rabbi in Reformed Judaism in the United States. In our very first conversation over a cup of coffee, we talked about our common last name and I said my great grandfather lived in Boston, and she said, "So did mine."

"What was your great grandfather's name?" she asked. I told her Conrad, but that he was known to everyone as Coon.

"Coon," she exclaimed, "He was my great grandfather's younger brother, but when he left our faith, the family lost track of him."

Rabbi Laura Geller is now rabbi of the Beverly Hills Synagogue and a board member of *Tikkun*, a liberal Jewish magazine. She sent me my first subscription. I still subscribe to it, but we have had no contact since our meeting in 1986. Tikkun is the Hebrew word for "make-up" or "mend," and can be translated as "transform the world."

Intent on his chosen work, my great grandfather quickly gave

Bob's love of gardens began early.

up the religion of his birth and embraced Roman Catholicism. His brother, on the other hand, remained a Jew and the two branches of the family have remained true to their religions to this day. I have distant Jewish cousins in Washington D. C. and California, and a couple of second cousins who are retired Roman Catholic priests.

My grandfather, Henry (Hank), worked for the railroad in Wyoming and came home once or twice a year to visit my grandmother, his Methodist wife, in Avoca, Wisconsin.

My dad, Frank Arthur Geller, grew up on a farm near Spring Green, Wisconsin. The oldest of eleven children, he left home before the youngest of his siblings was born. While he wasn't religious in a traditional way, and managed to avoid formal church affiliation all his life, the neighbors nicknamed him Santa Claus because he had a habit of quietly helping out wherever he saw a need. Every year he worked in the fields to get the crops in for a family who didn't have the health and manpower to get the job done by themselves. And they weren't the only ones he helped.

He attended Wisconsin Normal Training School and became a math teacher, football coach, and eventually a principal in Egan, South Dakota. It was there that he met and married Flora

Mandame Brennan, an elementary school teacher, recently returned from a teaching stint in a country school in western Nebraska where her brother was in the process of homesteading land. When her brother quit the land, Flo, as she was always called, took it over, but the time came when loneliness drove her back to her home in Egan where she met Frank.

In 1908, after they'd been married for two years and had their first child, Lucille Ann, they left Egan to prove up on the 320 acres in Simla, (now Mud Springs) Nebraska, available to them through Flora's brother. Mud Springs had been a pony express stop and lay in the panhandle of Nebraska between Sidney and Bridgeport. The wagon trail from the Black Hills to Denver cut through the east end of the homestead.

My mom worked hard, keeping house and feeding her family from her vegetable garden and with the chicken, beef and pork we produced on the farm, but she had an agreement with my dad that she would not work in the fields, and she never did. She didn't even milk the cows.

The four children that followed Lucille were all born on the farm: Roger arrived in 1918, Robert (that's me) in 1921, Charles in 1928 and Marjorie in 1930. My birthday is July third, though when the call came to the country doctor who was to deliver me on that day, I was considered something of a "fizzle" as my arrival had been anticipated on July Fourth.

Neither of my parents ever taught again after they moved to Nebraska, but instead worked the land and raised their five children. At first we lived in a primitive temporary dwelling with a well and no running water, and later in a two-story house ordered from Sears Roebuck. Our basement was dirt, but we had a cement porch on two sides of the house, and enough space for all of us to be comfortable. We had no running water until I'd finished college. The well was 60 feet from our house and one of our chores as kids was to haul water to the barrel in the kitchen where it was stored. When I was in high school, I remember the joy of a warm shower at the end of a long day in the field supplied by a contraption my brother and I rigged with a barrel

**Midwest Elementary School, sixth grade class, 1932.
Bob, front row, far right**

in a tree. The water warmed in the sun all day.

My parents were dryland farmers who grew corn, summer fallow wheat and silage, and raised pigs, cattle and chickens. Many of our neighbors were Germans from Russia, all of whom, with a single exception, owned their own land and homes.

Electricity was available from a private company if you could afford the cost of stringing line to your house, a half mile in our case. We waited until the REA (Rural Electric Association) made electricity available for most everyone in rural areas in 1946. Until that time we used "bright lamps" that had mantles and burned kerosene with a brilliant flame. Delco plants were popular on a few farms for generating electricity using batteries, and we also used coal oil lamps. I remember that one neighbor had a wind generator.

Our telephone was on a party line. Before you made a call, you had to pick up the phone to be sure no one else was talking. And sometimes you listened a little, to catch up on the local gossip. Each family on the party line was assigned a different ring for their phone. Four short rings meant there was an emergency

High school class, Dalton Nebraska, 1936.
Bob, top row, third from left

of some kind and everyone was to pick up and listen. It was like a 911 call is now. To this day, I think of ringing someone on the phone rather than calling, which has become the more common term. A call is when you call the pigs, a ring is for the phone.

One day my older brother Roger and I were playing in the barnyard roping pigs. Roger got a little too close to a boar that tore him open pretty badly. After she saw the blood and assessed the situation, my mother went to the phone and made an emergency call. Very soon a neighbor, who had a car, came to drive my brother into town. After some serious stitching up, he spent several days in the hospital recuperating.

More common emergencies in those days were grass or wheat field fires or agricultural accidents. Whatever the problem, it was good to know that there was a way to communicate and that there were neighbors around ready to help.

My dad bought a Chevrolet in 1928 so that we could make a trip to visit family in Iowa, South Dakota, and Wisconsin. We traveled at the end of August and into September so that I missed the beginning of first grade. For many years we used a team and

5

wagon to haul our grain to the elevator, and always traded some of our wheat for enough flour to feed the family for another year.

Other than the family trip to the Midwest, I didn't travel much. I remember one trip to Denver, a couple to Estes Park, one with the Boy Scouts, and, when I was 15, a trip to the Veterinary School at Colorado Agricultural and Mechanical School in our neighbor's truck. I delivered an ailing shorthorn bull of my dad's to the vet school for diagnosis. The news was not good. "That bull's no good," the vet said. "You can take it home and shoot it or I can shoot him for you right here." It didn't take me long to decide to haul him back home so that we could have the meat.

A trip to Washington D.C. for the World Boy Scout Jamboree in 1937 made a lasting impression on me. I earned the right to go by earning a great number of merit badges. I traveled by train to the biggest city I'd ever been in. I met boys from all over the world and we spent a week together, camping out and cooking our food. Our main course for dinner was provided by an army kitchen, but we cooked everything else ourselves, which turned out to be a good way to get to know each other. We all brought small trinkets from home to trade with each other and came home with caps, kerchiefs and wrist bands from all over the world.

We visited all the Washington sites, from the Lincoln Memorial and Washington Monument to the Smithsonian Institution and Monticello. A cousin on my father's side of the family had a husband on the White House police force who took me on a private tour of the White House.

When the week was over, I boarded a train to Chicago where I changed trains and traveled to Wisconsin to visit my fraternal grandparents in Avoca. I'd only seen them once before in my life. My grandpa was so deaf that the neighbors could always tell when he was home by the sound of the radio blaring as they passed by his house. I remember getting a 50-cent haircut in Avoca and my grandpa taking me to the butcher shop and teaching me about the different cuts of meat. He also impressed upon me the importance of getting to know the butcher and becoming his friend, something I never forgot. While I was in Avoca, I had my first official interview by someone from the local radio station who asked me about my experiences at the World Jamboree.

Sports

"He and I competed like crazy but often crossed the finish line holding hands."

The first pair of sneakers I ever owned came in the mail about two weeks after I won a quarter-mile running race barefoot, on a dirt track at the Morrill County Fair. They were a gift from Mildred Nelson, my first and second grade teacher, and they came with a little note that said, "When you get to high school, you're going to need these."

It had been five years since Mildred had taught me in the one room school about a mile from our farm. She knew I often ran to school and also that I owned two pairs of shoes — one for dress and one for work — and that shoes for play weren't in the family budget. Five years later, when I graduated from high school, she presented me with an Elgin watch and let me know that this was something I was going to need now that I couldn't just go by the sun to tell time.

I treasured that watch and it served me well for nearly 35 years. It got stolen once, from a counter where I left it as I peeled potatoes in the Hastings College cafeteria. But thanks to the forceful food service manager, Tilly Hoffmann, it was returned to me. When I told her it was missing, she said, "If you left it downstairs, we'll get it back." A co-worker confessed to picking it up, saying he didn't know who it belonged to. Unlike some of my co-workers, I liked Tilly a lot. But none of us who worked for her could have done anything but "fess up" when confronted by her intimidating presence.

The high school was five miles from my home in Dalton — too far to walk every day, or even to ride a horse. I therefore became a boarder, and during my four years of high school, I lived with three different families. For room and board, my family paid

High school football team. Dalton, Nebraska, 1935 — the year they were unbeaten and untied. Sophomore Bob, too small for the team that year, served as manager, masseuse and mascot. Front row, far left

these families five dollars a week and a quart of cream.

My track career continued at Hastings College where I specialized in the half-mile, mile, and two-mile. I was unbeaten during my senior year, running a 4:21 mile, good enough to claim the college record which held for two years. After I graduated, my deaf teammate beat my record. He and I competed like crazy but often crossed the finish line holding hands. He went on to become a journalist and worked for the newspaper in Scottsbluff, Nebraska.

Even though I loved football and basketball and went out for both in high school, I didn't go out for either in college. Instead I became one of four males on the cheerleading squad. The fun I had cheering on the Hastings Broncos with a bevy of 20 lovely young ladies far outweighed the occasional teasing I got for this extracurricular activity.

I always liked football but as a ninth and tenth grader at Dalton High School, I wasn't big enough to make the team. Instead I got into the action as mascot, which included everything from giving massages to carrying water to the players. By the time I was a junior, I finally reached five foot six, and the coach allowed as how I was big enough to play. I became the quarterback, not because of my extraordinary throwing arm, but because the coach knew I was the only member of the team who had all the plays memorized. My older brother, Roger, also played on the team and my dad was a loyal supporter at all our home games.

The coach, Mr. Roth, was also a science teacher. I developed a special relationship with him, partly because he was dating the physics teacher, who also taught my high school Sunday School class that met in the furnace/storage room of the Presbyterian Church. She liked me enough to invite me and my girlfriend to go to movies with her and Mr. Roth, who she was dating and later married.

I suspect she took a liking to me because I asked so many questions in class. She noticed that I could move through the material faster than many of her students and she never hesitated to give me extra work. I came to appreciate her ability to handle scientific questions in the context of faith. She taught me that science and religion are supportive of each other if we are willing to refrain from asking science to answer questions regarding faith. She was an important influence in my decision to enter the ministry.

My sophomore year we had a most incredible football season. In 11 games, in towns like Sidney, Kimball, Chadron, Lodgepole, Sunol and Peetz, Colorado, we were never scored upon. We made headlines in the sports pages of papers all over the state. I lettered twice in football and the team continued to have winning seasons, but never one like my sophomore year. I lettered in basketball for two years as well, but I was never tall enough to be a real force on the team.

During my years as a campus minister in Oklahoma, Arizona, and Colorado, I attended football games regularly and was often asked to give a prayer before the game started. (That's a tradition that has since gone out of style; in fact may no longer be legal.)

I was happy to offer a prayer, but more than once, it made me remember University of Texas coach Paul Bryant's response when he was asked if a prayer before a game did any good. "Sure," he said, "if you have the best team."

Student Geller at Hastings College, Hastings, Nebraska, 1941

College

"My God, you'll starve."

My dad's words turned the air blue the day I told him what I wanted to do with my life. He had a gift of profanity, though he never swore at people, only at things. One day, when I was in the field cultivating corn, my father brought lunch to me, and we sat in the shade of the tractor to eat. I was 16 and had just graduated from high school. He asked me about my plans.

"I want to go to college in Hastings," I told him.

"And what will you study?"

"To be a minister."

Bob, far left, in drama at Hastings College, 1941

"My God," he said, spewing a string of profanity until he ran out of breath, "My God, you'll starve."

My dad knew the local preacher well and knew that he, and all the preachers around, existed on meat, vegetables, fruit, milk and butter given to them by the local farmers.

"How will you pay for this education?" he asked when he'd recovered a little.

I explained that I had an opportunity to be taken "under care of Presbytery" by the Presbyterian Church, which meant that I had access to loans that I could repay with service.

My mentor, Kenneth Reeves, the Presbyterian minister in Dalton, grew up on a farm in central Nebraska and understood that a Nebraska farm boy needed to broaden his knowledge if he was to become an effective minister. "College will be a good start," he said, "but during your seminary years, seek out as many different experiences as you can." He also advised me not to major in religion in college. "You'll get plenty of that in seminary," he said. "Major in something else that interests you."

I took him at his word and majored in economics and speech and I've never been sorry. I learned enough about business and

Yearbook photo, recipient of the Bronco Award for best representing "constructive college citizenship," the highest award given at Hastings College. For the first time, in 1942, the award was presented to two people, Bob Geller and Betty Shehlsen, the first woman to ever receive it.

money so that I began to consciously save while a college student. My training in speech has stood me in good stead through all the years I've been called on to speak and lecture.

At Hastings College I earned my keep by working in the kitchen of a greasy spoon restaurant far enough away from campus that I had to buy my first bicycle in order to get to work. When the restaurant closed its doors, I moved on to a job peeling potatoes in the dining hall on campus. Work started at 6 a.m., and that was okay with me. There was a machine to partly peel the white potatoes, but I had to remove the "eyes" by hand. Sweet potato days were grim. You had to peel the cooked sweet potatoes by hand and you smelled like sweet potatoes for the rest of the day.

As a junior I "graduated" to a soft job in the college library magazine and resource room where I was free to study until I had a request for help or information. I had another job as an agent for a dry cleaner during three of my four years at Hastings. I collected clothes at the dorms, delivered them to the cleaner, and returned them to their owners, collecting a percentage for each delivery. In those days, we didn't have wash and wear clothes. Most of us mailed our clothes home to be washed and ironed.

I got to know a local politician who owned properties all over Hastings and often needed help maintaining them, for which he paid me 25 cents an hour. But at election time I hit the jackpot when he recruited me to hire students to hand out fliers outside the polling places. Each student got paid $5 and I got $5 for each student I recruited. Big bucks for those days!

During my college years many of our neighbors near the farm moved on, many to Colorado where they could raise crops on irrigated land. It was Depression time and my dad was able to buy up land that had been abandoned, to use as pasture and for summer fallow farming. I made money for college by renting land from my dad, planting wheat during the summer and harvesting it the following summer. I used my dad's machinery and he provided fuel in return for my help with his field work. Wheat prices were good between 1939 and 1941 and even though I paid my dad a third of my profits for use of the land, I usually had several hundred dollars by the end of the summer.

It was at that time that I began saving, just a little at a time, but regularly, a habit I continued through all my working years so that now, in my retirement, I have more money than I had access to at any time in my work life. I didn't work for it. The market did it all. Kenneth Reeve's suggestion to major in something other than religion turned out to make a huge difference in my life. I might add that when I graduated from college, I had more money than when I started, and I had no debt. It is true that tuition was only $300 a year, though at the time, that seemed like a huge amount.

My economics professor, Dr. Dykstra, was a gem of a teacher. From him I learned the history of economics, Marxist economics, and the national government's strategy of investing to get the economy going again. He was a believer in Roosevelt's New Deal. The most useful course I took from him was "Money and Banking in the Twentieth Century."

The year before I graduated, Dr. Dykstra went to the University of Nebraska where he continued as an advisor to the Roosevelt administration. Dykstra would bargain with his students at exam time by offering to give students a letter grade lower than they had earned up to that point in exchange for skipping the final. One of the few B's I received at Hastings College was in an economics class. I thought I had too many other things going on to cram for his exam which I knew would be very thorough. Looking back, I think he didn't like grading finals any better than students liked taking them.

Seminary

"If God is like my father, forget it."

I took Kenneth Reeves' advice and sought out a wide range of experiences while I was in seminary. I elected to spend an extra year in an internship before my senior year to broaden my experience even more, and became only the seventh person in McCormick Seminary history to do so. These days an internship is required of nearly all seminary students.

During my first year, I served a wealthy church in Lake Forest, Illinois where the minister was a scholarly gentleman, a Rhodes Scholar, and a classical preacher. Getting to know him and being exposed to the wealthy parishioners and their children began the broadening process for me. I served as advisor to the highschool group and had a chance to get to know them well, especially when we went on field trips together.

The summer after my first year of seminary, I assisted a Welshman in a Presbyterian Church in American Fork, Utah and got my first taste of Vacation Bible School. I'd never been to one but, nevertheless, I served as director, week after week, in small towns in the vicinity of American Fork. I learned about Mormons that summer as plenty of Mormon kids attended our Vacation Bible School. It was about the only activity available during the summer. We sang songs, played games, and I told stories, mostly parables, outside under the shade of a big tree.

One day in the little town of Payson, I told the story of the Good Samaritan to a group of intent listeners. I thought, this is a great opportunity, and so when I finished, I asked them what they thought the story meant for us and our lives. One little girl had a ready answer: "Your story doesn't mean anything to us because we're Mormons."

During my second year, back in Chicago, I served a second

generation immigrant population at Christopher House in Chicago. I spent time with highschoolers, getting to know them and coaching them in drama. Fortunately, my college speech major included drama and made me feel qualified for this role. Drama, I discovered, was a good way for these young people to find a voice and express themselves.

They played basketball as well and I often refereed their games. Years later, one fellow, who always called me "Gell" traveled to Stillwater, Oklahoma with his college basketball team when I was working on the campus there. I looked him up at halftime, and we were glad to see each other. The score was close, but ended in a loss for his team when, according to the referee, my Chicago friend's shot was put up too late for the basket to count before the final whistle. I saw him afterwards. "My shot was good, Gell, wasn't it?" he said.

"If you say so," I replied, "but I'm just another fan in the crowd and there's no way to protest the call."

The following summer I spent at Elgin State Hospital where there was a program designed to train hospital chaplains. I was in a full-time clinical training course and while I had no plan to be a hospital chaplain, the experience and exposure taught me much that was useful.

I elected to spend an internship year in Cedar City, Utah between my second and third year of seminary. My experience was sponsored by the National Board of Missions of the Presbyterian Church. During that time my connection with Mormons became closer and I learned an important lesson: The best way to live in Utah is to refuse to accept a minority status. My experience during this year had a strong influence on my choice of electives during my final seminary year.

Cedar City was a tourist town, close to Cedar Breaks and Bryce and Zion National Parks. There were more non Mormons there than in most towns in Utah, but still, the percentage was high. I credit June, who became my wife in December of that year, with instigating our increasingly close relationship with our Mormon neighbors. June had a beautiful singing voice and was often invited to sing in the Mormon Ward Houses. The parishioners began inviting June to sing at their meetings on Biblical theology and then began asking me to speak. We became good friends with the organist, a wonderful fellow, one of 71 children, son of a father with eight wives.

Before long I was giving lectures at Southern Utah State University in Cedar City. When the president, a Presbyterian, died, he was given an elaborate Mormon funeral followed by a Presbyterian service that I was asked to conduct. When it was over, it was obvious that even the Mormons present approved and I was pleased. My speaking duties also extended to a series of lectures at the Mormon Academy, an adjunct to the local high school.

I learned to fly fish that year with an elder in the Presbyterian Church who had a car. We'd take off on Saturdays and sometimes Sunday afternoons, and because meat was rationed at the time, we were grateful for the trout we caught. Despite the scarcity of meat, the local butcher, with whom I became friendly, never failed to provide meat, disregarding the necessary ration card, when my military friends came through town. It was his way of supporting the troops during World War II.

The war was made real for us in a different way by the presence of a Japanese internment camp in the desert, only 20 miles from Cedar City. Outside my assigned duties, I often visited the camp and tried to help the internees with needs they had that were not being met. The fact that very few of them were Christians made no difference to me. What I knew was that most of them were American citizens, and the fact that they were being detained was illegal according to our constitution.

During my years in the seminary, I made time to counsel at West Madison Street Mission, in Chicago. I also spoke often at the Illinois Juvenile Detention Center. Once I referred to God as "Father" and a young boy spoke up, "If God is like my father, forget it."

I returned to McCormick for my senior year with a wide range of practical experience. By this time I knew that I did not want to become a regular parish minister, but wanted to become involved in missions work — not necessarily overseas, but in churches that were not self-supporting, either because they were new, remote, or in underprivileged areas. In all my years in the ministry, I was never installed as a permanent parish minister; and I've never been sorry for that decision I made so long ago.

Paw Paw, Illinois

"That year I learned about rural ministry."

During my last last year of seminary I served a rural church in Paw Paw, Illinois, about 80 miles from McCormick Seminary. June and I and our small daughter, Gretchen, lived in Paw Paw. I commuted to school where I stayed Monday through Thursday, then came home to serve the church on weekends. This church, which was not self-supporting and therefore considered a mission, had a history of being served by seminary students. In return for my services I received a place to live and $100 a month. During that time Gretchen required some radiation treatment for a birth mark that cost $25 a month, leaving us $75 to live on. With a little help from June's parents, we managed.

That year I learned about rural ministry. The parishioners willingly shared their food with us. June did lots of singing at the church, directed a 60-person choir and conducted the youth group. She had plenty to do between caring for a young child, stoking the coal furnace below our apartment when I was gone, and keeping house with a small gas burner for a stove and a little portable oven which we set on the burner.

Our little apartment above a garage was cold and the wind blew in around the windows. There was no caulking around the windows until June's dad came to visit and stuffed newspaper into all the open spaces. His was a simple solution that helped a great deal.

West Virginia

"This is one of the best days of my life."

In 1946, following graduation from McCormick Seminary, I attended the summer session in Labor Temple on East Fourteenth Street in New York City, a controversial ministry of the Presbyterian Church formed to address the needs of miners and others who were in "industrial" work. In August, I went to work in the West Virginia Mountain Project that ministered to a string of 21 churches between Charleston and Beckley. This suited my desire to be involved with mission work and allowed me to see yet another aspect of the ministry. The project had seven staff members — five ministers and two Christian education workers who were not ordained. I was assigned to Ameagle and Dorothy, two small coal mining camps in the same valley. There was an operating mine in Ameagle, but Dorothy had been mined out; residents had to find work elsewhere although they continued to live in Dorothy.

I conducted two services in each town every Sunday, one in the morning and one in the evening. Saturday nights I conducted a service at a Pentecostal Church in which speaking in tongues was part of the service. (I called it "religious gymnastics.") Afterwards I conducted what I called bible study and the Pentecostals called a sermon. My days off in this mission came around only in months that had five Mondays.

June helped with the work as much as she could, teaching adult Sunday School and conducting the choirs. She had never taught adults before and had no experience with the conservative kind of religion we found in the valley, but she got along just fine.

The headquarters where June and I lived with Gretchen, were housed in what had been a Presbyterian boarding school. During the summer, June and Gretchen cleared out of the dormitory and went to stay with her parents in St. Louis, Missouri while I directed summer camps. To my delight, I received permission to institute the first camp experience for Black children. "We've thought about having camp for the Black kids, but just never got around to it," the director told me.

The summer conferences were co-ed and there were separate dorms for middle school and high school students. Boys stayed in one dorm and girls in another. For nearly all the children, it was their first overnight experience away from home, and they loved it. Music was a big part of the program, conducted by a blind staff member who was also a song writer and story teller. He had no sensitivity about the color of his students because he couldn't see them, but I did have a staff member ask me what we were going to do about the mattresses after camp was over. "We'll burn them if you'll buy new ones," I said.

The nine to twelve-year-old boys who came to the first all-Black camp in the summer slept together in a long dormitory room. Often they had a tough time settling down for the night. In order to facilitate their falling asleep, I began to tell them one segment of a continuous bedtime story that I made up each night as I went along. The stories were drawn from their local area. I remember weaving a yarn about the ghost who lived in an abandoned sawmill they knew about and who liked to play tricks on anyone who explored the old place. Once those boys had been lying down quietly for a very few minutes, they inevitably fell asleep.

I often walked the alleys in the little town of Dorothy, in hopes of making contact with people in the parish. All the company houses had back porches facing an alley. One day, as I came around the corner, there was a young grandma, probably in her fifties, sitting on her backyard swing smoking a corn cob pipe. The moment she saw me, she put her pipe away. A huge grin spread over her face; I've never seen anyone look happier.

"This is one of the best days of my life," she said. "It's the first day in 18 years that I haven't flown a white flag from that line over there." Her youngest of many grandchildren had just graduated from diapers.

The first funeral I ever conducted in West Virginia was for

a 20-year-old man who had committed suicide. He was a good young person who had attended church services regularly. Many of the people in that remote valley came from a line of thinking that said regardless of who he'd been or what he'd done in life, since he'd committed suicide, he would be going straight to Hell.

I thought for a long time how to best conduct this young man's funeral. For many years the Roman Catholics refused to conduct any sort of funeral for those who had killed themselves. I sensed some similar attitudes here. Even so, I anticipated a big crowd and I knew that the pall bearers would be the friends of this young man.

I began the service with a few introductory comments and a welcome to everyone there. Then, before I went any further, I said, "If there is anyone here who thinks he knows exactly what is going to happen to this young man, he should up speak now." Then I waited for two or three minutes. There was silence. I continued with the service, explaining as I went on that I felt that no reputable Bible scholar would take a single verse from the Bible and interpret it to mean that suicides were automatically doomed to live in Hell.

Afterwards the family, who ran a small grocery store and sandwich shop in town, let me know how grateful they were for my words. To this day I am in touch with a sister of the young man we buried that day so long ago.

Most of the people who lived in that small valley in West Virginia were strict, black-and-white, religious conservatives. Yet, among seven independent churches in a relatively small area, there was an amazingly wide range of opinion concerning the right way to perform a baptism. Some advocated face up, others face down; some demanded total immersion. Baptism by sprinkling was very rare. Some said still water could be used; others said only running water would work. Some insisted the person had to be immersed three times. As for me, I don't think any of those things make one bit of difference. I'm willing to baptize in the way that is most comfortable for the family involved. Usually, the baptizee has not yet formed a strong opinion on the matter.

Once after a revival in the Ameagle church, we had baptisms in the river. Baptism always drew large crowds. It was winter. One of the young coal miners who had become a Christian was rather well known for his rowdy and "sinful" life. After I baptized him he went up on the bank, someone put a blanket around him, and one young man in the crowd asked, "Jim, are you cold?"

Jim replied, "N-n-no."

"Put him in again, Preacher," the friend shouted. "He is still lying."

Bob photographed the calm of Hastings College campus the morning of December 7, 1941

Peacemaking

"Making war will always create conditions conducive to going to war again."

I was still in high school when I became acutely aware of what was happening to the Jews in Germany. The fact that the United States was unwilling to accept many of them as refugees made me sad and angry; I couldn't understand why my country wasn't willing to go to war to right this terrible wrong. I found an opportunity to express my feelings when a Nebraska congressman announced a statewide essay contest. I submitted my essay suggesting that the United States needed to get into the war immediately because of what was happening to the Jews. I won the contest and was rewarded with $25, a lot of money back then.

While I abhor war, I have never been a pacifist, and to this day believe that there are times and circumstances when war is necessary. At the same time, I agree with the Quakers who believe that making war will always create the conditions conducive to going to war again. A naval aviator friend of mine made sense to me when he pointed out that through World War II the

United States had batted 100 percent, winning every war we'd ever entered. Since that time our record has been one of dismal failure and defeat in encounters in Korea, Vietnam, Bay of Pigs, the Gulf War of 1991, which we did not win because we failed to oust Saddam Hussein, and the current war in Iraq.

Of course, the United States did enter the war following the surprise bombing of Pearl Harbor by the Japanese in December 1941. On that fateful Sunday I was announcing a radio broadcast of a concert at Hastings College when the station broke into the concert to share the news of the attack. Everyone knew it meant war. After the announcement I was asked to continue the program, which I did, after suggesting to the listeners that from this moment on music might be secondary in all of our lives for a long time to come.

When World War II ended, I was in a V-12 training program for chaplains, and at that time had the option to stay in the service for four years or get out immediately without any benefits, which I elected to do. During the war, while I was still in seminary, I did volunteer counseling with military trainees at Navy Pier in Chicago.

As the years went by, amplified by a philosophy class in critical thinking, my convictions about war became so strong that I took part in many peace marches during the Vietnam era. During the time I interned at Elgin State Mental Hospital when I was a seminary student, I conducted a case study that allowed me to see first hand the aftermath of war. The subject of my study was an army officer suffering with what today we'd call post traumatic shock syndrome. He was addicted to cigarettes but only allowed to have them when the hospital staff saw fit to hand them out. As a casual smoker, I began sharing my cigarettes with him whenever we spent time together. He was always grateful and we enjoyed smoking together as we talked. "Chaplain, why do you smoke?" he said to me one day.

"Hmm," I said. "To tell you the truth I can give you no good reason why I smoke."

"If I didn't have a good reason to smoke, I sure as Hell

wouldn't," he responded.

The next morning I went to work and avoided my first cigarette of the day. I haven't had one since. I remember this story, and I tell it here to illustrate how much I have learned by listening to the people I've come in contact with over the years. Listening is hard work, but it's worth the trouble.

Calling

"I never experienced a bolt from the sky..."

During the years that I've been a Presbyterian minister, I've often been asked when I received my "calling." For many of my fellow ministers, my answer has been disappointing. Unlike them, I never experienced a bolt from the sky offering a vision of what my life was to be like. There was no single moment when I felt a "calling" to become a minister.

Instead, my decision was first an intellectual one that grew and developed over time. The more experiences I had with people in the course of my work in the church, the more affirmed I felt in my decision to be a minister. I felt that the things I was doing were important; that they made a difference. My decision is continually confirmed each day of my life.

While I consider myself a conservative, there are those in the Presbyterian Church who call me a radical and at times have questioned whether or not I really received a calling. "I did," I tell them. "It's just different from yours." Then I'd go on to tell them the story of the man who saw a vision in the sky — letters that read "P.C.", and he interpreted them to mean "Preach Christ." Then I'd go on to explain that in the farm country where I come from, they'd be just as likely to mean "Plant Corn."

Over the years, I've been asked to serve as a parish minister several times. I made the decision to be involved in missionary work a long time ago, and I've never been sorry. In the early sixties, I had an opportunity to apply to become pastor of the First Presbyterian Church in Fort Collins. I had taught college-age students there, was familiar with the church, and knew many of the members well. June and I talked it over and decided that I had found my niche working with university students and that's where I should stay.

I was once introduced to the minister of a large Presbyterian church, (I won't say where.) who commented to me, "I've never met a campus minister I could trust." And he never did.

For many years in my ministry, most of which were in higher education, campus pastors were considered not quite as "real" as pastors in churches. Scores of times I've been asked, "When do you plan to get your own church and be a traditional pastor?" I know how to be one as I have served five times as a supply pastor for a few months. I was supply pastor at Stillwater Presbyterian Church, Stillwater, Oklahoma; Trinity Presbyterian Church, Tucson, Arizona; in Colorado at Westminster Presbyterian Church, First Presbyterian Church in Fort Collins, and at the Presbyterian Church in Masonville, Colorado.

In the National Campus Ministry Association made up of four to five hundred members, most never expected to make campus ministry their life's work. Only one Presbyterian minister stayed longer than I.

Campus ministry has been very rewarding to me, more than I ever dreamed it would be. It has taken me and my family to places in the world we might never have gone and allowed me to participate in academic life in ways I never would have experienced otherwise. If being a campus minister is in some way "coming in second," then so be it. It has been the best for me.

Theology

"You can find an argument for most anything except murder and mayhem in the Bible."

My theology is pretty simple. I believe in the importance of listening; in the value of silence. I'm a student of the Bible and I can play "Bible Baseball" (where you toss verses back and forth to each other) with the best of them, but I affirm the versatility of the good book. You can find an argument for most anything except murder and mayhem in the Bible. One of my most serious objections to fundamentalists is that they pick and choose their verses to the exclusion of others that don't agree with their line of thought.

I have a difficult time with ultraconservatism, because of its exclusivity. If one doesn't believe, right down the line, the way fundamentalists do, it's a closed shop. I have seen the Presbyterian Church become increasingly conservative in the past decade; sometimes I find it discouraging. But I've never considered leaving the church because I believe strongly that there needs to be a voice to support the reform church and to encourage individual thinking. I believe in the validity of differing points of view and the possibility of coexisting comfortably with those who hold different convictions.

Many times in my life I have heard the question, "Are you saved?" I usually responded with, "Get out of the past and read Paul. Biblically, I am *being* saved daily and I hope you are also."

Life as a
Campus Minister

"I'd never thought of college work as missionary work."

My experience during three summers of working with college and graduate students in West Virginia opened the door to campus ministry for me, though I didn't realize it at the time. When I was getting ready to accept my first "real job" as a minister, my high school mentor, Rev. Kenneth Reeves, was serving as Director of Christian Education for the Presbyterian Church. It was he who suggested that I consider campus ministry. At the time, I'd never thought of college work as missionary work. I'd assumed that I'd go overseas to serve international missions or work with small new churches who were not yet self-supporting (home missions) in the United States.

Oklahoma Agricultural and Mechanical College

My first campus assignment in 1949 took me to a land grant school, Oklahoma A and M, in Stillwater. In the years following World War II, denominational ministries were developing on campuses all across the country. The Oklahoma organization was housed in a wing of the Presbyterian Church and billed itself as "a home away from home" for college students. As time went by that function grew to include preparing students for life beyond school. During my six-year tenure, the school grew from 10,000 to 15,000 students and our organization grew as well.

When I began my career at Oklahoma A and M, I assumed that I'd be limited to working on campus. But it didn't take long to become aware of needs in the community, and I found myself establishing the first senior citizens' group in Stillwater. A little later, we welcomed Alcoholics Anonymous (AA) to our campus house for their meetings. Because of a brother and uncles who had problems with alcohol, I was especially interested in this organization.

Within a year after they moved in, AA asked me to address their national meeting in Salt Lake City, Utah. One evening the topic of conversation got around to coincidences, and thoughts kept rattling around in my head. Before I went to sleep that night, I jotted down a one-liner that went like this: "Coincidence may be God's way of remaining anonymous." That was in 1953. To this day, those lines appear in AA literature although they took the liberty of changing the words "may be" to "is."

Part of 1954 is a blur for me, due to the fact that I spent three weeks in the hospital with an appendix that had ruptured — probably because it had entwined itself around part of my large intestine and diaphragm. "We took an octopus out of you," I remember the surgeon saying.

I also remember the Disciples of Christ minister visiting me in the hospital every day. During my stay, I made sure I had plenty of quarters on hand to activate the radio in my room so that I could hear Metropolitan Opera performances on Saturday afternoons. We made great friends in Stillwater. While many of our contemporaries from those days are not living, we still hear from former students now and then.

University of Arizona

A Presbyterian minister who had observed my work at Oklahoma A and M was aware that the campus ministry program in Tucson was in decline and asked me if I'd be willing to take it over and resurrect it. I agreed to try, but insisted on living in a private residence rather than the campus ministry house where quarters were provided for the minister and his family. We rented a house for three months, then bought one on Poe Street (I liked that name.), and finally built a home when we needed more space for our growing family.

At the time, the University of Arizona had 15,000 students, but it was well on its way to a growth spurt that saw it swell to 20,000 students by the time I left. It was known as a school for upper and upper middle class kids, quite different from Oklahoma A and M whose student population was far less wealthy in most cases.

At Arizona, a controversial philosophy professor was notorious for his antireligious attitudes and his determination to share his point of view with students in classroom lectures. Some students had complained to the department head, but nothing had ever been done to curtail this man. One year, I planned a strategy that had a surprising result. I recruited four particularly bright students, three men and a woman, to take his class. Then I got a copy of his course synopsis, and every week I met with these students and coached them on questions to ask the professor.

They started during the first week of class and badgered the professor until he was desperate. Finally he told them: "If you keep asking questions, I'm going to kick you out of class."

"Then we'll report you to the dean," they replied.

But at the end of the term, the professor wrote an exam unlike any he'd ever written before. It contained no hint of his bias. He had come to a conclusion on his own about the way he had been teaching. In the end he was able to let his students know that their questioning had helped him to become a better teacher. I couldn't help feeling a sense of satisfaction for this happy, nonconfrontive resolution of the issue, even though I knew I had been more than a little interfering. I must admit, it was great fun!

Years later I met up with this professor at a conference in Fort Collins on philosophy, history, and faith presented by the CSU Faculty Christian Fellowship. I was surprised at his presence there and concluded that, perhaps, somewhere along the way, he may have had a change of heart or mind.

A Faith that Asks Questions

I was asked to respond to one of the lectures at this conference and the theme of my talk revolved around my conviction that the most dangerous combination throughout history has been an alliance between faith and the state. This sort of alliance is dangerous to faith and dangerous to the state. When it occurs, the faithful are convinced they have the right to govern the state. The state, with faith on its side, believes its actions to be ordained by God. The results of this kind of thinking are usually disastrous.

I like a faith that always asks questions. Faith ought to be as open as outstretched arms, and there should be acceptance of the fact that not every question will have an answer.

Work/Service Projects

*"Lord, we thank you for getting us so tired
doing this kind of work."*

From my first job as a campus minister in Oklahoma until I retired from Colorado State University in 1990, I've been a strong advocate of work/service student projects. They are among the most meaningful aspects of a campus ministry program and provide memorable times for everyone involved. There's something about working together for the benefit of others that makes it possible to build community among strangers in a very short time.

During Spring Break at Oklahoma A and M in 1953, I took a group of 12 students across the state to Sallisaw where we were to build a small medical clinic for the Choctaw Indians. It was agreed ahead of time that a crew of Indians (We didn't call them Native Americans back then.) would be part of our work party. Days one and two went well, and the college students were enthused about their work. On day three I went to the site early to look things over and decide what we needed to do next. When the students arrived, our Indian crew members had not yet showed up. "Let's get going," one student said. "We don't have much time to get this project done."

"No." I said. "We'll wait for the Indians." When they failed to appear, I insisted that we leave the site and take the day off. We spent the time enjoying ourselves in and beside a nearby creek. We did not return to the job until the next morning.

The next day the Indian crew showed up on time and we worked together that day and for the rest of the week. None of them mentioned their absence of the day before, nor did they offer any explanation. I knew just enough about the way Indians think to know that if we'd worked without them the day before, we'd never have seen them again.

In 1954 I took a crew from Oklahoma A and M to the little town of Ranchos de Taos about six miles south of Taos, New Mexico, to paint and repair a Presbyterian mission preschool. The job wasn't hard and we had lots of good help from the local people. Since one purpose of the trip was to get to know a new place, we stopped work early one day and went into Taos to visit a few of the many art galleries in town. In one gallery I made the innocent comment that the paintings were all in the same brown tone and had a certain sameness about them. I also said I thought they looked like photographs and looked quite ordinary to me. Before I knew it, one of the owners, who with her husband had painted the pieces, and who had overheard my remarks, threw us all out. I guess she figured we were only a bunch of students and not likely to buy anything anyway.

The following year, my first at the University of Arizona, I took a group to Mayaguez, Puerto Rico for a month to fix up and paint a neighborhood house and to build a cinder block chapel in a nearby rural area. The old u-shaped mission where we stayed had lots of mosquitos. When we arrived we were offered nets for our beds which I refused because I'm not much bothered by mosquitos. But when the maids came to change our sheets, they insisted I have a net. When I wondered why, I was told that whenever a mosquito bit me in the night, I'd roll over in my sleep and leave a blood spot on the sheet. After that I slept under a net.

One day I was trying my best, in my halting Spanish, to speak with an eight-year-old boy. He listened for a while, then looked at me and said, "Why don't you just speak English?"

We had Sunday and a consecutive day each week to travel. When we visited the Presbyterian Agricultural Mission, we were invited to attend the wedding of a couple who had been together for many years. At the time they fell in love, they didn't have the money demanded by the Catholic priest to marry them. So, on this day, we witnessed their marriage as did their children and grandchildren.

Another memorable trip was to the south coast of Puerto Rico where the ocean is filled with phosphorous. At night, from the deck of our small boat, we marveled at the luminous water and schools of glowing fish as they swam by.

A few weeks before spring break of 1955 we journeyed to Sells, Arizona to build a small medical clinic for the Papago Indians. Before we began our work, we met with the local tribe members to plan what we'd do. We talked and talked, discussing each detail at length. It seemed we were in agreement. "Good," said the students. "Now we're ready to come back and do the job."

"No," I said. "Not so fast. All we did was agree that we'd talked about what we were going to do. When it was obvious that we were not yet at a starting point, the students wanted to know how I knew that. "Well," I said, "you have to listen carefully. And you have to know about Indians and the way they do business. First they talk about it. Then, they must meet again to formalize the agreement."

During that trip I had a chance to get to know a small group of people who were translating the Bible from English into their native dialect. They had been trained by the University of Oklahoma branch of the National Bible Translation Training Center.

One year, University of Arizona students spent their spring break rehabilitating Montlure, an old conference center in the mountains of northern Arizona. The work days started early with a few readings each morning followed by long hard days scrubbing, pounding nails, and painting. Our goal was to have the center ready for the summer season. After supper, which we cooked for ourselves, I was surprised to see how early these young people headed off to bed. I'll always remember one young fellow who said the prayer before the evening meal. "Lord, we thank you for getting us so tired doing this kind of work."

Work service projects were an important part of my work at CSU as well. One year we built a medical clinic in the San Luis Valley in southern Colorado; another year Jim White, the assistant campus minister, and I split into two teams. He took a

41

group to Chicago to do painting and repairs in the inner city, and I took a team of painters to inner city Denver where we worked on the sadly neglected Manual High School. In the course of our work, we became well acquainted with the neighborhood and the people who lived there.

Closer to home, we became involved in weekend projects in Andersonville, Buckingham and Spanish Colony, now called Alta Vista — more politically correct I suspect, in northeast Fort Collins. Because it was close to the sugar beet factory that needed a water supply, Spanish Colony had running water, but the other two areas did not. Marcielle Wood, a Fort Collins benefactor, gave us a home she owned in Spanish Colony. We named it Viva House and repaired it so that a couple of students could live in it. With donated books they established a library for the neighborhood and ran it out of Viva House. They also conducted an after school program in the house.

One year, when spring break fell during Holy Week, Jim White and his crew had the unenviable task of cleaning out the septic tank at the Viva House. I was working with my crew to haul away all the old cars and other junk from Spanish Colony. It so happened that Jim was scheduled to speak at a Holy Week service at First Presbyterian Church. He and his crew came directly from the job, looking, as the church business manager put it, "worse than a bunch of dirty hippies."

When the business manager complained loudly to me about their appearance and how disrespectful he felt it was, I asked him if he'd heard Jim's message. "No," he answered. "Well, that was the important thing," I said. They could have showed up in their swimsuits for all I cared.

Jim, who was much younger than I, had a hard time getting beyond thinking that I was his boss. I wasn't. We worked closely together and we both answered to the board. I did lobby the board to ensure that he got a raise every year.

Buckingham Park is located on ground between Buckingham and the Poudre River, once owned by the Great Western Sugar Company. They had just closed the sugar beet plant and their land was an unsightly patch of weeds, trash and junk illegally dumped there. The sugar company agreed to lease the land to the city for $1.00 a year and City Council agreed to the lease but did not see a way to finance a park for several years. Eight students cleaned up the area on their own and enlisted the help of the National Guard to grade and smooth it. Service clubs donated playground equipment, and the park opened in 1964 with a ball field and children's play area, but no grass. When we asked the city to bring water to the area so we could plant grass, they explained that there was no way because there was no main water line near enough to provide enough pressure to water the park.

Parks and Recreation began using the field for ball games. Our college students began a campaign, writing letters to the newspaper, City Council, and Parks and Recreation, to get the city to bring water to the park, to no avail. Then one day, I ran into H. R. Phillips, then Parks and Recreation Director, who had just finished Spring Creek Park, complete with a sprinkling system. "I guess we just don't have enough pressure," I said to him, and that's all I said. A month later a water line was laid to Buckingham Park.

Another spring break, CSU students traveled to Tucson to paint a neighborhood center in a slum on the south side of town. It was connected to a Presbyterian Church, the first church in the nation to provide a refuge for Mexican nationals. The church was prosecuted, but eventually won its case when the Supreme Court agreed they were not breaking the law.

But before the Supreme Court decision, the church was often swarming with police and FBI. While it was not law, there was a long-held principle in effect that said no one could ever be arrested in a church. The officers abided by that principle, but made every attempt to arrest the illegals when they emerged from the church.

With the help of United Campus Ministry crews, another house owned by Marcielle Woods in Buckingham became the third home of Volunteers Clearing House, now the Education and Life Training Center. This building also housed the first office of the Neighbor-to-Neighbor program. Junior high and highschool tutoring programs were conducted there as well.

One of our crew that year was a young man from the Cameroon, who June and I sponsored. On the day we took a trip across the border into Mexico, he couldn't go because of visa restrictions. But he went everywhere else with us — on camping trips, to the home of June's parents in Colorado Springs, and to my parents' fiftieth wedding anniversary in Nebraska where he definitely turned some heads. Some of my relatives could not understand why I'd bring a black person to this family event.

He left CSU with a degree in electrical engineering and returned to the Cameroon where he became head of all electric systems for his country. He and his wife, a lawyer, have six children all of whom have graduated from college. One came to visit us recently.

Ghost Ranch, the Presbyterian camp and conference center on the Chama River near Abiqui, New Mexico was our work/ service destination in 1957. This 20,000-acre spread was donated to the Board of Christian Education of the Presbyterian Church by a layman and his wife from Tucson. I was on the team that made the decision to accept his gift and turn it into a camp and conference center. We took a bus load and a car load that year; and our crew included two high school students, my son, Tim, and Nancy Graves, a Fort Collins girl. The rest of my family went along as well and vacationed while the crew repaired fences and buildings. It was so hot, dry, and windy that we made the national news that week as a place with zero humidity. We drank gallons of water and despite our hard work, we didn't sweat.

West Africa

"...the new flag of Sierra Leone was raised as the new national anthem of the independent country boomed out."

I had been in Tucson, as campus minister at the University of Arizona, for five years and had a strong program going when I got a call from Margaret Flory in New York. "How would you like to go to West Africa for a year?" she asked.

I'd always hoped that one day, when my children were older, we'd have an opportunity to serve overseas. I figured most any assignment I'd be offered would be for three to five years. But it certainly wasn't something I'd been hoping or planning for in the near future. I'd been fully engaged in creating a viable program at the University of Arizona and had become quite active in the community as well. It was plenty busy at home too, since our fourth child and third son, Vic, had been born only a few months before.

Still, I was curious enough to listen to what Margaret had in mind. She worked for the Presbyterian Board of Foreign Missions as secretary in overseas higher education and also as a recruiter for the Presbyterian National Campus Ministry that had a program to send campus ministers abroad. They needed someone to replace the person who did leadership training and to serve as a traveling secretary for the Student Christian Movement (SCM) overseeing SCM sites at secondary schools (called colleges in West Africa) and two universities, Forabay College in Sierra Leone and the University of Liberia in Monrovia. I would be based in Sierra Leone for 11 months, August 1960 through July 1961.

The minister at Trinity Presbyterian Church in Tucson where I did much of my campus ministry work had been in Africa several times and had a soft spot for the place. He encouraged me to go. A couple who were doing graduate work at AU and were living in the campus ministry house agreed to curtail their graduate work for a year and take my place. He was a Presbyterian minister and she a Christian education worker, so they were ideal for the job. It wasn't hard to find a family to stay in our house for what it cost us to do so. (The people who lived in our house bought a freezer during that year which we use to this day.)

In preparation for our move in the summer of 1960, June packed up the children and moved in with her parents, then living in Colorado Springs, while I took a month to attend the World Christian Student Federation conference in Strasbourg, France and then take a short course in international economics at the London School of Economics. When the time came to go to Africa, June and the children went to New York where they stayed in Margaret Flory's apartment for a few days. A University of Arizona graduate student met them in the city and gave them the grand tour before they boarded a plane for Dakar, Senegal.

Gretchen, nearly 15, was a little reluctant to go at first. She was at an age when it was difficult to leave school and her friends. Mark, ten, and Tim, six, were up for the adventure. Vic, barely a year, wasn't consulted. June's dad, who had always been extremely supportive of us, thought that perhaps I'd gone a little crazy this time.

I arrived in Dakar one day before the family. After their arrival, we spent two days in a hotel before we boarded a plane to Guinea, a country then controlled by the Soviet Union. We were not allowed to leave the airport while we awaited our flight to Freetown, the capital of Sierra Leone. In fact we had to get special permission and have a military guard in order to find a place where we could warm up a bottle for little Vic. I'd never before been in a place patrolled by soldiers with their machine guns at the ready.

After our arrival at the Freetown airport, we boarded a small ferry to cross the river into town. It was the rainy season, and sure enough, it was raining. Our ferry, a small launch, was covered, but there was no room for me under the roof. As luck would have it, I'd left my umbrella behind in Dakar. I was out on the deck in the rain and fog. Soon it became obvious that our driver had lost his way because of the poor visibility. Fortunately, he spotted the lights of another boat who could guide him to Kissy Dock where we disembarked. The senior advisers for SCM met a bedraggled replacement for the leadership trainer and traveling secretary and his family.

We were escorted to our lodging, one half of a double unit that had been a recovery hospital for the British Navy during World War II. Two Brits, one an architect/engineer and the other a teacher, lived on the other side of the unit. The structure measured 140 feet long and 50 feet wide with concrete floors, an iron roof, but no outside walls or windows. There were screens, some fine enough to keep mosquitos out, while others, called "hail screens," kept out only larger creatures. The living spaces were constructed inside this large outer shell which formed a porch around the building. The bathroom, shower and kitchen, were lined up along one side of the building.

We had brought no furniture, only bedding, linens, and cooking utensils. We were provided with mosquito nets for each of our beds because of the constant threat of malaria. Some SCM friends loaned us enough furniture to get along.

Gretchen had a room of her own. The two older boys shared a room, and Vic had a small bed in our room. We had running water, a bathroom with a shower, a small gas cooking stove and a food safe, but no refrigerator until we bought our own. We had to boil all our drinking water as is common in so much of the world. Privacy was at a premium; there were curtains only at the bedroom window screens.

During our time in Sierra Leone, we traveled quite a bit in the used Volkswagen Beetle we bought there and sold when we left. And yes, the six of us fit, although Tim usually crammed himself into the small space between the back seats and the engine. When we took longer trips, we traveled with other people who were willing to squeeze a Geller, usually Gretchen, in with them.

There were only eight white girls in the Anglican school Gretchen attended. Wearing a uniform was new to her and the first day of school she showed up in her straight green cotton dress, but with a fancy petticoat underneath that made the skirt stick out. When she was told that such petticoats were not allowed, she came home and announced that she wanted to go home and live with her grandparents. The moment soon passed and Gretchen adjusted quickly to her new surroundings.

She played the piano well enough that she was soon in demand, not only at her school but at the U.K. Methodist Girls College where she was recruited to accompany the choral group. She became proficient in Patwa, the travel language of the country, a mixture of English, Portuguese, French and native dialects. She fit in quickly, and made friends from all over the world whose parents were in business, the diplomatic service, teachers in missionary schools, or medical missionaries.

Gretchen was the only one of us to contract malaria, and she suffered through the chills and sweats not once but twice. Because she had been taking preventive medication, both bouts were mild. She recovered quickly with no lasting effects. When we boarded the mail boat bound for England after our year in Sierra Leone, most of the people who came to the dock to see us off were Gretchen's friends. They brought so many gifts we had trouble dealing with them in our cramped quarters.

As the oldest of our children, Gretchen was perhaps most influenced by our time in Africa. The boys have some memories and occasionally talk about schools and the friends they made, both black and white, but they have never returned.

In the fall of 1967, after she had graduated from college, Gretchen and her husband went to Ghana with the Peace Corps. She taught high school science and he taught art. They traveled through much of East and Central Africa during their two years there, an experience they might never have had if she hadn't spent a year in Sierra Leone.

The boys attended the international school and studied under the British system, which emphasized math at an early age. Tim found that he was way ahead in math when he entered the second grade back in Arizona. Both boys learned to play soccer that year.

Their school wasn't big enough to field a team, but they played informally after school. The boys' school was out at 12:30, which left them long afternoons for sports, climbing trees, and reading. Gretchen's school got out later and she often played the piano for the Methodist Girls College chorus until late afternoon.

The native people were fascinated by Vic, a blonde, curly-haired little boy they couldn't get enough of. I loved getting to know these friendly, outgoing people and learned a little Patwa myself, enough so that I could get along on our travels. Many of our trips involved a ferry ride across the river. Often we had to wait for the tide to come in before the ferry could operate. It was during these times that I enjoyed chatting with the locals. I got to know some chiefs among the 14 tribes in the country. They spoke English, making it easy for me to converse with them.

Armed with a basic medical manual given to me by a doctor friend, I served as medical man for the family and watched for symptoms with the help of my book. Luckily we stayed healthy except for Gretchen's malaria and hepatitis, which Vic, and later June, contracted. We journeyed to the interior of the country to seek help for Vic at a clinic run by a woman doctor — surprisingly enough — from Nebraska. She quickly diagnosed his symptoms, but there was no helpful medication at the time. The prescription was to eat well, rest and wait.

June's case was more severe, necessitating a week-long stay in the hospital in Freetown shortly before we left the country. Gretchen and I packed up our things for the 10-day ocean journey to Liverpool. We were careful not to mention June's recent illness as we boarded the ship, for fear that we wouldn't be allowed to travel.

Even though I'd booked passage six months ahead of our departure time, I had to buy first class tickets in order to accommodate all six of us. That turned out to be a good thing. We had a spacious cabin and the run of the ship, which included a small swimming pool and a badminton court. It was the first time I'd ever seen badminton played. We felt a bit limited because we had to eat with the first class passengers, but the rest of the time we associated with everyone. The ship made a stop at the Canary Islands. There the children were thrilled with camel rides. We also encountered traders peddling their goods and bought souvenirs from them.

Many of the treasured items in our home today came from our year in Sierra Leone. Street sellers often came to our house, as did the barber who cut my hair. We shopped at an outdoor market and also at a shop, somewhat like a supermarket, where we could buy canned meat and vegetables. It was almost impossible to get rid of the taste of the disinfectant we had to use to make sure fresh vegetables were safe to eat, so we resorted to canned vegetables. Bananas and mangoes grew in our yard. Eggs were available, but there was no fresh meat unless the mail boat had just made a delivery. Cattle and sheep were not raised in the country because of the prevalence of the tsetse fly.

We ate lots of fresh-caught fish, purchased at the dock from fishermen. We bought our bread fresh-baked from small bakeries and carried it home wrapped in newspaper. Only canned milk was available. We ate lots of long grain rice, bought in huge bags, which we shared with our friends and neighbors. It had to be carefully washed before cooking.

We paid Sam, our houseboy, 13 British pounds a month and that made him the best paid houseboy in town. Out of my 100-pound-a-month salary, 30 pounds went for rent, and the rest for incidentals. At the time, a pound was worth about $2.50. Although most families employed a guard, we could lock our house and decided to do without. From what we could see, guards spent most of their time sleeping and carried only a "tief" (thief) stick, probably not too effective in case of a real emergency. We did employ a man who came to "brush" (cut) our grass with a sickle.

Our neighbors came from Ireland, Scotland, England and Italy. Most were business people, a few were teachers. Several of them lived in houses similar to ours that had been recovery hospitals for the sick and/or wounded members of the British Navy. We lived in the flat part of town, not as cool as the hill close to a small mountain range that formed a backdrop for the

Sam, our houseboy in
Freetown, Sierra Leone,
with his family, 1961

city, where the university and hospital were located. I still have a slide I took of buzzards sitting on the roof of the public hospital in the center of the city.

In addition to visiting each of the SCM sites in Sierra Leone and the surrounding countries during my stay, I organized a leadership training conference in Freetown to which participants came from all over Sierra Leone and neighboring Liberia. The goal was to teach campus ministry leaders techniques for making them successful in their work with young people. I taught some of the sessions and also called upon the faculty of Forabay College in Freetown, where the conference was held, to share their expertise.

Aside from sharing practical advice and addressing issues facing SCM ministries in West Africa, the conference gave participants the sense that they were part of a regional movement thriving in several African countries. We subsidized the conference so that anyone could afford to come. For a fee of three pounds, we provided food, lodging, and instruction.

Freetown got its name because it was the city where potential slaves rescued from ships the British intercepted at sea were brought. Along with their freedom they were given English names and assigned to European families so that they could become integrated into the culture and eventually get an education. In Freetown there was a huge baobab tree where the slaves were delivered and their bonds removed. They were assigned to families to begin the acculturation process, which included learning English. The British abolished slavery before any other European country or the United States, and intentionally intercepted ships at sea in order to free the slaves they carried.

During our time in Sierra Leone, we witnessed an historic event: the advent of the first Peace Corps volunteers in the country. I remember greeting them and thinking to myself how very green they appeared to be.

I was moved by my visit to a Leper Colony in Liberia. I observed people in different stages of the disease and was impressed by the treatment they received. It seemed that the young people who were affected received especially good treatment. The colony, a small village isolated from the outside world, was supported by the government. It was clean, well-organized and well maintained. Residents were allowed to have their families come to visit, but were not allowed out of the village. At that time and in that place, doctors weren't sure about how leprosy was contracted, and they were taking no chances.

Much of rural Africa had no electricity during the time we lived there. That meant no access to radios. In some places only a few people owned watches. Adherence to specific times meant nothing to the people. Travel crises that made it impossible to keep time commitments intervened so frequently that most people felt no pressure to be "on time" the way we do in the West.

When I visited schools, students knew ahead of time that I was coming but they never knew when until the moment I showed up. Then someone would be sent around to announce that it was now time for the promised SCM meeting. As I observed the way

Women dancers from Guinea celebrate Sierra Leone's independence, 1961

all this worked, I began to realize how "wound up" about time we westerners have become.

A Palava House in every town provided a place for the men to gather and talk. The women were too busy caring for the children and working in the fields, so it was the men who came together to gossip and share the news. Many of the older adults spoke in one of the 14 dialects in the country, but the younger men often conversed in English. I enjoyed listening to them. Usually there was one person who had access to a radio or somehow learned the news, and could share with others. African countries were in the throes of becoming independent in those days and much of the talk revolved around those enormous changes.

The really big event of the year occurred in May 1961 when Sierra Leone ceased being a colony and became independent. A whole week of celebration included music, street dancing, feasts, speeches and a night of ceremony with diplomats, dancers and the official dedication. In a darkened stadium, fireworks like I've never seen before exploded, followed by the playing of the British national anthem, "God Save the Queen," and then the lowering of the Union Jack. In a stirring finale, the new flag of Sierra Leone was raised as the new national anthem of the independent country boomed out. What a night it was!

A delight for me and for my family was living close to the sea. My wife and children had never even seen an ocean until they embarked on this adventure and I had never spent much time near the sea. Lots of weekends Sam, our houseboy, packed us a picnic lunch and we took off to spend the day at the beach. The children loved the ocean and couldn't get enough of the surf. Usually on our way home, we stopped at the dock to buy fresh seafood, another treat for us. There's something about living by the sea that gets on the inside of a person, and you never get rid of it.

The climate took some adjusting for us. Sierra Leone is eight degrees above the equator so the temperature does not vary much in the course of a year. What does vary is the rainfall, from 140 inches in the rainy season to sometimes no rain at all during the dry season, which can last four or five months. The rivers dry up. The ferries stop running, and people and animals alike suffer from the lack of moisture.

In November our family welcomed the Harmattan winds that come all the way from Norway bringing a respite from the heat. We laughed at the reaction of the natives as they bundled up against "the cold." These winds are in reality hot and dry, but they feel cool because they provide relief from the humidity.

On Friday mornings June and I watched the members of the small Muslim community giving alms to the poor. A group of men gathered on a corner of the outdoor market and gave away coins to anyone who came — from crippled people riding in the back of a truck to anyone who wandered into the area knowing that on this day they could get a hand-out.

On many Sunday afternoons, I preached at the prison in Freetown. When I learned that there was no minister in town visiting the prison on any sort of schedule, I began to go quite often. Sometimes I took Gretchen and Mark along.

To my surprise, I discovered that the prisoners were the most literate population to whom I preached, with the possible exception of members of one or two of the area churches. This was because so many of the prisoners were incarcerated for

Typical laundry day in West Africa, 1961

stealing, an opportunity available to them only because they were educated enough to hold good jobs where they associated with people who had money and possessions. For many at that time, stealing was a way of life. The prison was a bleak place with no library and no books to speak of. By the time we left, a small library had been established and I donated many of my books to it before I came home.

Today Sierra Leone, devastated by a 10-year civil war, is ranked the poorest country in the world, despite the diamonds found there. Rebels took over the alluvial diamond fields and used the gems to finance the war, aimed at taking over the existing regime. The rebels finally lost their struggle after the intervention of United Nations and African Union troops.

While we were in the country, a medical doctor with whom I'd become acquainted became Secretary of Foreign Relations for the newly independent country. He did a fine job, ably assisted by his wife, an American Black woman and a born diplomat. They met when he attended medical school in Boston. His wife became quietly involved in many humanitarian undertakings in Sierra Leone. When things began to fall apart and war was imminent, this man and his wife returned to Massachusetts where they lived for the rest of their lives.

Before independence in 1961, all shops, schools, and government offices in Sierra Leone closed between 12:30 and 2 p.m, a custom no doubt adopted from southern European countries. Until then, I'd never lived in a place that observed siesta time. I thought then, and I continue to think, that it is a great practice. After independence, shops, and eventually schools and government offices, began to stay open during those hot noon hours. My friend the Secretary of Foreign Relations apparently shared my feelings about siesta time as he expressed his disappointment at the passing of this custom. "You Americans have ruined our world," he told me.

Living so close at hand with extreme poverty made re-entry into the United States extremely difficult for me. I couldn't adjust to what seemed to me an elitist university setting, and I had trouble re-integrating into the community where I had been quite active in the past.

Moving On

"From the beginning, Fort Collins felt like home."

Perhaps because my time in Africa resulted in such a major shift in my perspective, when I was offered a chance to interview for campus ministry jobs at the University of Colorado in Boulder and Colorado State University in Fort Collins, I didn't hesitate. These offers were made only a year after our return, but something inside told me it was time to move on.

One interview at the University of Colorado was enough to make me realize CU wasn't the place for me. I think they felt I wasn't intellectual enough for them, and I didn't feel I'd be a good fit either.

My good friend Bill Hage, minister at First Presbyterian Church in Fort Collins, encouraged me to interview at CSU, and I wasn't disappointed. I met with the Westminster Fellowship of Westminster House, and we soon came to an agreement. At that time Tom Sutherland, who would later spend six years as a captive in Beirut, Lebanon, was the treasurer of the board.

By August, 1962, the six of us arrived in Fort Collins with not a piece of winter clothing among us. Fortunately, June's father was still in the clothing business and helped us out with some cold weather gear.

Because campus ministry was still seen as "a home away from home" back then, and the house was set up to accommodate the minister and his family, we moved into the campus ministry house at 629 Howes Street. But we had not been accustomed to living in campus ministry houses and stayed only until we built a home of our own where we lived until 1980.

By this time I was a veteran home builder, having built my first house in Stillwater, Oklahoma where I had to borrow the down payment from my father-in-law's bank in Hastings,

Nebraska. The banker I went to see in Stillwater said, "I thought ministers always lived in housing provided by the church," and then decided I wasn't a good risk. After building a 1400 square foot house with three bedrooms for $11,000 and selling it a few years later, I had enough money to buy a house in Tucson which I sold when we needed more space. I then built a house that accommodated our family of six. We lived in it for only a year before going to Africa, and one year after our return.

From the beginning, Fort Collins felt like home and Colorado State University was a place I understood. Because it had been Colorado Agricultural and Mechanical College until 1957 and was a land grant school, it had much in common with Oklahoma A and M, my first campus ministry assignment. Like Oklahoma, CSU had veterinary medicine, forestry and engineering schools. In those days, Oklahoma A and M even used the Pingree Park mountain campus of CSU for its summer forestry camp because they had no suitable outdoor campus of their own.

CSU was small, about 9,000 students, when I came, and more suited to me than the University of Arizona with 20,000 students. It was a good time to come, and although I didn't know it then, the town was about to explode, and the university along with it.

United Campus Ministry History

"UCM was one of the largest religious organizations on campus."

In its earliest days, United Campus Ministry was housed in the First Presbyterian Church and was a mission of the Presbyterian Church, supported by the national church. Leroy Loats was hired in 1948 as a designated campus minister to serve the students of Colorado State University.

In 1952 First Presbyterian Church asked the synod to purchase the present property at 629 South Howes Street, a home built in

Bob and associate campus minister, Jim White, pose by the United Campus Christian Fellowship sign. It later became United Campus Ministry, and is now the Geller Center for Spiritual Development.

1912. The following year an addition was built and later when the house to the south burned, the synod bought that property. Hillel, the Jewish student organization, occupied space in the building in 2007, but has recently purchased its own property.

The original concept was to provide living quarters for the campus minister. Leroy Loats lived in the house with his wife and three children, as did his successor, who took over the position in 1956. By that time, UCM was one of the largest student religious organizations on campus. It functioned as a small church, asking students to become members and make pledges. However, it never became self-sustaining. There were as many as 75 registered members, out of a student body of five or six thousand.

The second campus minister was academically oriented and his career goal was to become a college teacher. During his tenure, he provided intellectual stimulation for the students, but it soon became obvious that they needed more, as membership began to dwindle. He eventually accepted a position in a Presbyterian college in Illinois where he remained for the rest of his career.

So many weddings

When I arrived on the scene in 1962, UCM was still organized as a "make believe" Presbyterian Church, but within three years that changed. In 1964 the official name of the organization was United Campus Christian Fellowship, but that name was short-lived. A strong national student movement was de-emphasizing the differences between denominations and promoting ecumenism. As a result, by 1965 the organization was no longer Presbyterian alone, and by 1967, in order to comply with a national name change, it became United Campus Ministry, a name that more accurately represented a campus organization that was serving a wide range of students, some Jewish, some Mormon, and others not traditionally considered "Christian."

During that time, many local churches who'd been maintaining campus organizations dissolved them and became part of UCM. Among them were the American Baptists, Disciples of Christ, Congregational Church, (now United Church of Christ), First Christian Church, the Mennonite, Episcopal and Methodist churches. For a time the national Presbyterian Church paid my salary, but gradually the Colorado Synod took over that role and eventually the local churches who participated in UCM all made contributions.

Camps and Conferences

"I dreamed up more than one gimmick to keep the members of that age group busy..."

Camps and conferences at Highland Presbyterian Camp and Conference Center near Allenspark were a significant and successful part of my ministry in Colorado. For more than 50 years I directed camps for sixth graders through college graduates as well as several summer camps for senior citizens and for grandparents and grandchildren. But it was the camps for junior high kids that brought out my creativity. I dreamed up more than one gimmick to keep the members of this age group busy every moment, the only way to avoid problems.

I remember once at Highland Camp a few rowdy campers stayed up until the wee hours the night they arrived. I found out who they were, routed them out of bed at 5:30 a.m. the next day and made them hike up a long hill and back before breakfast. We didn't hear from those boys again after bedtime!

As a member of the camp's board of trustees for several years, I was able to accomplish some things that had long term influence for the camp. I negotiated with the state of Colorado for adjudication of the wells and spring on the property, which was the source of water for the camp.

When the owners of two summer homes adjacent to the property became too old to use them, I suggested that in exchange for the free water from the camp that they'd had access to for 30 years, they might like to donate their homes plus a strip of adjoining land, to the camp. They agreed, making it possible to enlarge the camp and protect the south side of the property from encroachment by potential new cabins.

I was also able to facilitate acquisition of the Salvation Army Camp on the east side of the property. Through gifts and purchases, Highland Camp grew from 40 to 165 acres in those years.

Associates and Volunteers

"She could make anyone feel welcome."

Tom Nadelin, my associate at UCM between 1978 and 1985 was a native of Germany but his English was so impeccable it was impossible to know that from his speech. In the years following World War II, he had been recruited by the American Air Force in Germany and had spent two years serving with Americans. During this experience he perfected his English and adopted a distinctly American accent.

Tom was an independent thinker with an incredibly creative mind. He came to UCM with a Masters of Divinity from a Congregational seminary, now UCC Seminary, in Chicago. One of his most creative efforts in Fort Collins was the cabaret he put on twice a year for the community. Participants were students, faculty members, and townspeople. Among them were John Kefalas, Dan Siegfried and a very tall Italian fellow, Paolo, who taught math at a university in Italy. The cast was a happy blend of talented people who put their heads together to create an entertaining and provocative satirical show, making fun, in comment and in song, of teachers, students, townspeople and politics. In 2006, many of them returned to Fort Collins for a reunion and made a memorable CD souvenir of their time together. UCM supported their efforts from the beginning, with funding for a performance venue and money for advertising the event.

Tom had his career ups and downs in the years after he left Fort Collins, moving from Massachusetts to UC Davis in California, and working as a counselor and organizer for Hospice. He now lives in St. Louis, Missouri where he has developed a class in pastoral care for the elderly, specifically those with Alzheimer's disease, at a Congregational seminary. This is the first course of its kind to be offered at the seminary and is an area not addressed in many seminaries.

When I look back over my years in the ministry in Fort Collins, I feel compelled to recognize and give credit to lay folks for their great help and leadership in getting so much done. Among the standouts were Marcielle Wood, Fran Thompson, and Martha Armstrong all of whom encouraged the women they knew to develop programs in the community.

More than 100 CSU students have served as student directors at UCM, living in the house, maintaining it and also devoting time to UCM programs. Married students Dave and Carol Shanks stand out as the best housekeepers ever. Under their contract each gave two hours a week toward maintenance and spent another hour each week conducting programs. I want to mention seminary interns, Scott Howard, Carol Fox and David Buss, and Jack Rowe, who served as director for the international student houses.

I could not have managed without associate staff like Jim White. Louise Cordsen, my secretary for nearly a quarter of a century, was never full time, but turned out an unbelievable amount of work. She could decipher my handwriting and get letters, newsletters, and reports out — always on time. For many years volunteers kept the office open in the afternoons. The most memorable of these was Charlotte Kanode, who was blind and who came to work with her dog. She could make anyone feel welcome.

The Friday Morning Book Group

"We were so intrigued with The Ghost Dance *that we discussed it for three months."*

In November 2007 the Friday Morning Book Group turned forty. While it's probably not the oldest book group in the area, its members can take credit for showing up faithfully every Friday morning at 7 a.m., except during July and August.

I'd been involved with book groups when I worked as a campus minister in Oklahoma and in Arizona. When I came to Fort Collins, I became involved in a couple of CSU faculty groups, the Danforth Fellows and a Faculty Christian Fellowship organization. By 1967, these groups were winding down and there seemed to be a void.

That year I began the Friday Morning Book Group and while the membership was always open to anyone, during the early years all members were men. Today the membership is fairly evenly divided between men and women. Roughly 15 to 20 people attend regularly.

The intention of the group was to read in all the academic disciplines, getting around to each one perhaps every other year. We read in philosophy, journalism, history, biology, botany, political science, theoretical physics, and delve into works on war and peace. In order to determine the best books for us to read and, with limited time to do so, I developed what I call "diagonal reading," a method of scanning a book by reading topic and closing sentences for most paragraphs. I've found that if the writer is good, it's easy to get the gist of the work this way. This process serves me well to this day.

From the beginning, we've met in the basement of the UCM house, now known as the UCM/Geller Center for Spiritual Development, at 629 South Howes Street, close to the CSU campus. Coffee and juice is provided, and members take turns

Bob shares a list of more than 500 books read at the 40th anniversary of the Friday Morning Book Club, 2007

bringing breakfast food. Over time we experimented with noon and evening meetings, but the early morning time seems to suit everyone best.

We meet for an hour and finish in time for people to get to work. With the passage of time, fewer members are working and the retired among us often linger for an extra half hour or so. We usually spend three to five weeks on a book, but sometimes longer. We were so intrigued with *The Ghost Dance: Origins of Religion* by Weston La Barre, that we discussed it for three months. Bob Zimdahl, Professor Emeritus, Bioagricultural Sciences and Pest Management, a faithful longtime member and avid reader, still rereads *The Ghost Dance* every couple of years because it has so much meaning for him.

I usually start the discussion and then try to keep it on track. Some members speak often, others not so much, but when they do we're all likely to listen with special care, and benefit from their words.

In honor of the group's becoming forty, KUNC, Greeley, Fort Collins, and Steamboat Springs public radio station, featured the Geller Center as a sponsor for the day, celebrating the fortieth birthday of the radio station and the book group.

Second Career

"I got the job, but not before I answered some questions I thought were a little unusual."

My 35 years as a part-time chaplain for Woodward Governor Company in Fort Collins ran concurrently with and 10 years beyond my tenure as a campus minister. When I arrived in town in 1962, Woodward Governor was a small company with perhaps 250 employees housed in a building near downtown Fort Collins on Riverside Avenue. When Bill Hage, my friend and the minister at First Presbyterian, left town and gave up his job as part-time chaplain at Woodward, I applied for the position for a couple of reasons: the chaplain concept was familiar to me, and I needed the additional income to educate my family. I got the job but not before I answered some questions I thought a little unusual: Did I drink? "Moderately." Did I smoke? "No longer."

The job suited my schedule well. Summer was the busiest time at Woodward, and the load was lighter then at UCM. In the summer, new recruits came on board at Woodward, and I conducted classes for them. Later I offered classes for retiring employees. As the company grew, I began to spend a half day a week throughout the year counseling employees. I was on call whenever they needed me and over the years performed many funerals and weddings for Woodward families. Often, I was the only connection they had with any formal religion.

This unique company also employed a lawyer, a banker, a doctor and a barber for use by their employees. They had an extremely conservative philosophy, but they cared deeply about those who worked for them.

Woodward paid me well and, in addition, took care of the lawn at my house for 17 years. When that benefit came to an end, they were kind enough to raise my salary to compensate.

Well, I did make a suggestion to that effect, and they agreed.

I made regular rounds at Woodward, touching base with as many of the employees as I could, working to maintain an ongoing relationship with them. I became part of their rituals: when, after two years on probation, employees became "permanent;" when they were acknowledged for 25 years of service; and when they retired. When Woodward opened an academy for young summer interns, I taught a course, and for more years than I can count, I've given the opening prayer at the semiannual meeting of the 25-year club.

When I was gone for a year to work on a graduate degree at Menninger's Institute, I found an appropriate replacement, but when I left for New Zealand, the minister I was exchanging with was found wanting — his hair was too long — so someone else had to be recruited. When I spent a second time in New Zealand, this time 18 months, I was able to find a replacement with an acceptable hair style.

Once, during the days when coats and ties were dress code at Woodward, I showed up for a company photo wearing my trademark bolo tie. When they sent me home to change to something more appropriate, I returned wearing a clerical collar atop a purple shirt. No one said anything and the photo session commenced.

When I formally retired from my job in 1998, I was presented with a plaque and a clock to commemorate my years at Woodward. To this day, I often perform funerals and weddings for Woodward families. After a recent service, a man came up to me said he wanted me to conduct his funeral. "I'm a good bit older than you are, and that may not be possible," I said.

"Couldn't you put it on tape?" was his reply.

Graduate School

*"Menninger's is a unique institution and my year
of study there added a new dimension to my
counseling work at UCM."*

The more time I spent in my job, the more I realized how
much I could benefit from professional training in counseling.
In order to get this training, I took a sabbatical year in 1968
to study at Menningers' School of Psychiatry, then in Topeka,
Kansas, now in Houston, Texas. Dubuque Theological Seminary
and the Division of Religion and Psychiatry at Menningers' had
a masters degree in sacred theology — STM. It required summer
classes at Dubuque. I graduated in 1972 with the STM.

Menningers' is a unique institution and my year of study
there added a new dimension to my counseling work at UCM.
The school recognized the need for a program that encompassed
religion and psychiatry. It was a great place for learning, facilitated
by three methods: case studies with a small group and supervisor;
classroom lectures; and field work requiring detailed reports
every two weeks.

The students in my program were ministers, some in the
process of changing careers, others there to enhance the work
they were doing. Among my fellow students were two nuns, a
Jesuit priest, and several Protestant ministers. One man from
Holland needed training to enable him to develop a counseling
program in prisons in his home country. It was possible to become
certified in either social work or counseling.

The school was also unique in the approach they took
towards students, most of whom were older and had families.
They acknowledged the presence of spouses and children and
provided activities for them. Our two older children were grown
by then, but Vic spent his fifth grade year there. Tim became an

immediate hit when he won the ninth grade tennis tournament soon after his arrival and also played the bassoon — a rare skill in those parts. At the end of that year, Tim stayed in Kansas for a month and went to Lawrence where he participated in the music school summer program at the University of Kansas.

At Menningers' I learned about the relatively new concept of including the whole family in counseling. When I returned to Fort Collins, I became the first person to introduce family counseling to the community and the university. The technique is difficult because the counselor must be constantly alert to all kinds of small clues from the participants — from details such as where they sit to how they interact with each other.

Eventually this method of counseling became popular among other counselors in town and at the university. The College of Applied Human Sciences established a family counseling course and I often taught sections of those classes. In addition, I had a student from the program that I supervised every year. During all that time I had at least one family in counseling continuously — some for as long as three years.

The counseling I did with engaged couples I called premarriage education, being careful not to call it counseling. In those days I didn't hesitate to give couples lots of homework. These days, since I work for nothing, the homework has become less burdensome — for them and for me.

After I completed my certification at Menningers,' we had a staff of three at UCM. We divided the duties and counseling became my responsibility.

New Zealand

"In a way, the place has become our second home."

By 1976 I'd already been away from my job as campus minister for two extended periods, one in West Africa, and then for my graduate training at Menningers.' We had built a "year away" into our program at UCM, so in 1976 I began to search for an exchange. I wanted an English speaking country and a place where I had not been before. After making some contacts in Hong Kong, Australia, and briefly considering the Philippines, I learned about a counseling center associated with the Presbyterian church in Christchurch, New Zealand whose director was interested in leaving for a year.

My certification in counseling made the job seem like a good fit for me. The traditional exchange arrangement at that time was to exchange houses, jobs and salaries. My counterpart had recently been divorced and had no home, so the church board found us housing. He moved into our house, received my salary, which was twice what he'd been making, and took over my duties including keeping the Friday Morning Book Group alive. As I mentioned earlier, he wasn't acceptable as chaplain at Woodward Governor because his hair was deemed too long, but a suitable replacement was found for that part of my work.

The job that I accepted as director of the counseling center was overseen by the Social Work Division of the Presbyterian Church. My duties included seeing clients, conducting staff meetings, and speaking to groups in the area.

The home that the board of the church found for us belonged to a professor and sat on a hill overlooking the ocean. Our two older children did not accompany us, but Tim entered Canterbury University in Christchurch and Vic did his third year of high school in New Zealand.

Maori Meeting House, 1976

Tim's time "down under" convinced him to take up a career in music. One rainy day he was offered a ride to school by a man who happened to be the director of the Christchurch symphony. Perhaps he picked Tim up because he was carrying a bassoon. "We have an opening for a bassoon player," the director said. "Would you be interested in trying out?"

Tim not only got the job, but by the end of the year had become assistant director of the symphony and was conducting rehearsals. He stayed in Christchurch for as long as his visa would allow, grateful for his background and interest in music that had made his time in New Zealand especially meaningful.

Vic tried out for the high school rugby team, knowing nothing about how to play the game. He made the team and earned the right to travel to Australia during spring break to compete with schools there.

Through a contact of mine, Vic was invited to spend six weeks on a farm where he learned to herd sheep on a motorcycle and formed a lasting friendship. The sheep farmer, Malcolm Cone, who later earned a Ph.D in international relations and became a college professor, kept his farm when he moved on to an academic career. We have maintained a friendship with this man, his wife and children, and have hosted them in Fort Collins.

View from the Geller's deck, Christchurch, 1976

The New Zealand experience gave me a chance to do lots of things I liked. I enjoyed supervising the counseling staff and the chance to become involved in the community. Because Christchurch was the jumping off point for American Antarctic expeditions, people often mistook me for an explorer or scientist, and that was fun.

I treasure the relationship I developed with Peter, the Dutch minister of the small church on the hill that we attended. He had a colorful past which included activity in the underground during World War II, helping people to escape from Germany to England. He was lucky to come out of that alive. After the war, he and his wife and six children emigrated to New Zealand. When he retired, Peter entered law school and became the oldest law school graduate of Durham University. After graduation he went to work for a law firm, but took no fees, an idea I have adopted since retirement. I no longer charge for the counseling I do, and the arrangement provides me with great freedom.

Return to New Zealand

I felt strongly that when I retired in 1990 after 28 years in campus ministry at CSU, it would be a good idea for me to disappear for a while. I suggested to the board that they hire an interim, and take their time selecting my successor, but that didn't happen. They offered the position to Jeff Borg, a Methodist minister who stayed in the job for three years. As hard as I tried to get out of the way, I found I could not get out of people's heads.

Immediately after I retired, June and I took a three-month trip to visit friends around the U.S. After six weeks back home, we left for New Zealand for 15 months. This time I was to share a two-church parish with a minister who was already there, but was quite new to the ministry. Because I was retired, I planned to offer my services as a volunteer. I received a house and a car for what was supposed to be part-time work. With my co-minister, I served churches in the Maori town of Otaki and in Waikanae, a small retirement community with a golf course and nice beach.

The other minister and I divided up the duties, but I soon found my part-time status difficult to maintain. I started off preaching twice a month in each church, but my associate ran into difficulties and I found myself doing more. I solved this problem by agreeing to work full-time for two months and then taking two weeks off so that June and I could travel. That arrangement worked well.

Our children were grown and out on their own by this time, but Vic did come to visit for a month to tour the north island and to see his old friends. This time June had more free time to become involved in women's groups in the church, which was a pleasure for her. I started a weekly study group, did lots and lots of calling in both towns, and presented a four-part lecture series as part of the Kapiti Coast Lecture Series offered by the Otaki/Waikanae Presbyterian Church. New Zealanders are serious about continuing education, and I found this series of talks to be very popular.

We enjoyed learning about the fascinating Maori culture and noticed a different outlook among people who for a long time had been quite isolated, as islanders reachable only by sea. By 1991 many people from the South Pacific Islands had come to the area because of the availability of jobs — and this influx had an influence on the society as well.

June and I set off on our eighth journey to New Zealand during the writing of this book in September 2007. Both of us anticipated the trip with great pleasure. In a way, the place has become our second home. Following our 15 months at Otaki and Waikanae, we were invited to return twice for three month periods when I did storytelling. We were able to see the new Otaki Church that I had helped to plan when I was there. June and I had a beautiful pulpit made for the church using salvaged wood from the Kairi tree, now a protected species on the island. We also gave money for fans to circulate the heat in the building and made a contribution to an informal area now known as the Geller Lounge in the church.

We continue to correspond with about 70 different people in New Zealand, and saw many of them on our month-long journey.

The text of the final lecture I gave in the four-part series, Theology for a Planetary Pilgrim: Doing Theology in the Twenty-first Century, follows. The talks were given on Monday evenings July 8 through 29, 1991. The New Zealand (British) spelling is used.

Theology for a Planetary Pilgrim: Doing Theology in the Twenty-first Century

A few words are in order about the theme of this series and a bit of summary of the journey thus far. The words of the theme were chosen deliberately. Pilgrim brings up the image of going somewhere — a journey. One of the characteristics of a journey is that landscape keeps changing all the time. This certainly should be typical of the journey of faith. Doing suggests to me responding to the landscape during the journey. What have we seen thus far on this journey?

1. We began with what I think is an essential perspective for a Christian doing theology — a Biblical memory system against which the choices and decisions of daily life are made.

Perspective does make all the difference in the world. Another illustration about the difference is from an American humourist and essayist, Robert Benchley. When he was a student at Harvard University, one of his questions on examination was about a dispute between the U.S. and the U.K. over fishing rights and international waters. The students were asked to discuss the dispute from the perspectives of the U.S. and the U.K. Benchley wrote: "I know nothing about the point of view of Great Britain and I know nothing about the point of view of the U.S. Therefore, I shall discuss the question from the point of view of the fish." There is a great difference. I am convinced that a Biblical memory does provide an essential difference when I do Christian theology.

2. We then moved — journeyed — to how to make appropriate use of the Biblical and faith symbols — words and objects common to our faith — and the need to keep the symbols transparent. Illustrative symbols were Bible, Church, Worship and Christian. We are to see, hear, feel, taste, smell our way through the symbols to the concepts that are the reason for inventing the symbols — words — in the first place.

3. What is the landscape like on the journey? Several things could have been chosen — I chose the area that is inescapable in terms of our present situation and the one that I think will have a great deal to do with our future, even to the extent of possibly ending life on the earth as we know it now. The major aspect of our journey is science and scientific technology or applied science. The scientific paradigm — perhaps still emerging — that I chose was Chaos Science — sometimes just called "Chaos." It is in

many minds the most current science and it clearly impinges on us in easy to recognize ways. Chaos Science is for the common people as well as for the professional scientist. It is somewhat reassuring to know that no matter what, there is this cosmic glitch, cosmic untidiness — an inexplicable hiccup in the order, an unpredictability, a mutational inclination, a simple to complex phenomenon and a complex to simple one as well. All the while entropy persists and in some way all the factors work to anchor mystery and wonder in the centre of being. The wonder is as much in the cell and the smallest of particles as it is in the largest of universes. Randomness seems present in both the micro and macro universe. Chaos Science observes and studies process and notes that nature won't hold still. It studies that which is still becoming. That has a ring about it that sounds strangely like aspects of theology.

My conviction is that faith cannot live unless it finds a way of relating relevantly to the scientific world of its environment. I used pantheism as a parallel to Chaos Science. Pantheism affirms that life will not hold still. Everything in science and scientific technology is a source of learning something about creation and us creatures. Thomas Haldane, a great British entomologist, was once cornered at a party by an over pious, conceited clergyman who addressed Haldane loudly, "And tell me, Dr. Haldane, what has your life work with insects told you about God?" Haldane quietly replied, "that the Creator has an inordinate concern for beetles." Some of you know that there are so many kinds of beetles that not all have been classified along with their being the most numerous insect on earth.

Some of us think that since our daily life is chaos much of the time, that we are quite in tune with the paradigm of Chaos Science, and more importantly, the Christian affirms that science without faith is easily neutral or amoral about the uses of science. The misuse of science can and does threaten survival. A quiet observation from Biblical memory says that humans can and will misuse things and that the better a thing is for humanity, the more likely it will be misused. The poet Christopher Frey writes of this when he wonders how it would all end, and he said it might not end in a big bang like many people think, but in a final whimper. Biblical memory reminds that God will not destroy us, but it does not say God will stop us from destroying ourselves.

When I was a young lad in secondary school, I wrote a short satirical story that was published in the "Great American Bible," the Reader's Digest. It was about the last war on earth. After all the colored races had been destroyed, the whites got into a war to the finish between the freckled people and the unfreckled. The war was waged so effectively that there remained one freckled woman and an unfreckled man. They decided to call off the war, make a truce and eat a meal together to celebrate. When they were about to begin, the woman went to the stove to get something that had been prepared for the meal and while her back was turned the man shot her dead. Then he sat down to the table and ate the soup she had poisoned. Then there was peace!

Pantheism affirms that God is in everything, everything is in God, but they are not identical. This seems quite clear to those who are aware that they are on a faith journey — as a pilgrim. Both theology and science are fundamentally an awakening of the profound sense of mystery. In this world of scintillating objects, ideas and events jumping out from all directions and in all shapes and sizes, Hyers asks in The Comic Vision, "When is the last time you said, "Wow!" The ordinary world is not very ordinary.

That brings us to a "theology for survival." If you had known I was going to give the foregoing summary, you could have skipped the first three sessions. "Never mind," as you folks say — so let's get on with it.

A Theology for Survival —
Standing Outside Ourselves

Survival has many dimensions. Certainly one of the most obvious dimensions is the earth — cosmic survival. Will the earth survive as a viable ecological and life sustaining environment? The problems are global and the interconnections of billions of parts are challenging. Pollution of air and water, contamination of every conceivable kind, radioactivity, fossil fuel supplies and consequences of use, erosion of top soil, over population, depletion of rain forests, loss of important species, all point to one of the few species in all nature that regularly fouls its own nest. No other species is in the position to foul the nest — the earth — with such devastating portent. Also, no other major species fouls its social environment as does homo sapiens.

There have been two common responses to the environmental and ecological threats. One places a blind faith in scientific technology that will save us when things get really bad. The other is equally inadequate, a misled faith that God will intervene and save the earth, and even if God doesn't, it will be alright for Christians because they will be in heaven! No. If the earth is to be saved from destruction, it will be saved by humans. Biblical memory says that's the way God created the earth. It may be as simple and small as picking up some litter, saving some water, turning off a light, or as big as banding together with millions of others to change the practices of raping the earth. Nothing less than personal and corporate concerted action will reverse the present trend toward devastation and desolation.

What planet earth is like in the last decade of the 21st century will not affect you physically, but personally it is a major concern because of your great grandchildren and their children. It is a real concern for the serious folk like Green Peace members and ridiculous ones like the 600 members of the Eternal Flame Foundation meeting in Scottsdale, Arizona, U.S.A., who believe that since they have the death coding genes, they will live forever. Given present trends in the earth's environment, one wonders if their style of life 100 years from now will have even the faintest resemblance to the super rich, posh amenities available in Scottsdale for their meeting.

Then there are also the personal and individual dimensions that are upon more than a few of us at this moment. There are many close at hand issues: health, accidents, natural disasters, depression, oppression of others, refugees, abuse, incest, hunger, family disintegration, and of course, this week, The Budget. Even on that one, perspective makes all the difference in interpretation. To borrow the Robert Benchley words, there is the perspective of National, the perspective of Labour, and I think the point of view of the fish. I talked to a man in a dairy store last week who was unimpressed by all the Budget hype. He knew for sure that none of it is as important as the All Black-Wallaby Rugby test this week. However, quite apart from the humourous aspects, there is the very grim and, to some, hopeless scenario, and I think it is the height of folly for Christians in particular to respond by, "Just have faith in God. It will be alright. Leave it to God." I think "faith in God" means it is over to us! That's a big part of what the incarnation is about. The atheist says, "It's hopeless." The Christian says, "God has a hope and showed us in Jesus how to get on with the Kingdom work." A world renowned atheist once lectured eloquently about the human hopeless situation and used the metaphor of life that consisted of humans on a raft in a great sea. It was only a matter of time until man was finished off by a storm, thirst, disease or starvation because human life is absurd and has no purpose. A thinking member of the clergy heard the metaphor and said, "I just refuse to get on that damned raft." I choose that course of action too.

However, as we "get on with it," it is quite important that we get our assumptions clear. An illustration reminds us that it is of great importance to check our assumptions. A couple immigrated from Europe to the U.S., the mountainous state of Colorado. This woman and man brought with them their taste for wild mushrooms and the expertise to recognize the nonpoisonous ones. In late summer the mushrooms are just right

81

for gathering and so they went to the mountains and gathered a great abundance. Back at home they dried some, froze some, ate many and decided to share their wonderful harvest with some friends. They invited three couples to a mushroom feast. The hostess prepared mushrooms in several ways and they all had a great feast. In the course of the dinner, the hostess went to the kitchen and dished up a special casserole. What wouldn't fit into the serving dish she scraped into the cat's dish on the kitchen floor and the friends resumed their repast. When they had all eaten and drunk their fill, they gathered up the dishes to help with the wash. When they went to the kitchen they found the family cat stretched out on the floor, writhing and crying. The host immediately called the doctor and told what had happened. The doctor said that poisonous mushrooms were not to be fooled around with and to meet him at the emergency room at the hospital. There all eight of them went through the gruesome experience of having their stomachs pumped. It was a chastened group that rode, almost in silence, back to the house. As they entered the driveway, the host exclaimed, "Oh my God, I completely forgot about our cat." They rushed into the kitchen and there on the floor, found the cat with five new kittens. (Adapted from: *The Outrageous Mustard Seed*). If the task of survival is left to us, then we'd better check our assumptions about the Bible, the source of the essential perspective.

Assumptions about the Bible are different from those in science. Science posits a theory and then sets out to prove or disprove it with either logic or reason or from empirical data. The Bible is not a statement of conclusions but a statement of presuppositions. To treat the Bible as though it "proves" the truth is to both misunderstand it and to judge it by alien processes. Proof belongs to the realm of scientific verification. The characteristic "logic" of the Bible is confessional, assertive, unargued, e.g., the Bible does not examine creation and conclude that God is creator. The Bible does not review Israel's history and conclude that God redeems. The Bible does not probe the history of the church and prove that Jesus was raised. Those methods are common to the assumptions of science and common to how many Christians try to use the Bible. The Bible asserts that God is creator and then draws derivative statements about creation and about our stewardship. The Bible confesses that God redeems and then asserts what that means for history and that it is going somewhere. The Bible affirms that Jesus is raised and then makes claims for the church and resurrection style of life.

Bible study uses different epistemology (way of knowing). It is not scientific. The premises (assumptions) of Biblical faith start the other way around. Proof is not an essential ingredient of faith. The central substance of Biblical memory is not based on proof but in the courage and sureness of witnesses who dare to bring testimony. That testimony (witness) is in the posture of confession, not proof. The central substance of the Bible is "Kerygma," (proclamation) not anything proven. It is just declared.

The authority of scripture is not based on an assumption that it is a "library" of proofs, but on a faith — decision to take seriously the voice of faith heard and seen through the test. It does not ignore our scientific or ordinary experience. The assumption is that all experience of learning is a part of the wonder of creation and incorporates the paradox of suffering and glory in the mystery of God. Perhaps an even greater act of faith is the realization that part of the mystery of God is that survival is turned over to us. The scriptures are a bit like Chaos Science in that they continue to surprise us. Pantheistic theology assumes the surprises. (The original meaning of Panthesis is, "God is in all the forces of the earth."

There are two very important questions related to survival. They are personal questions. They are illustrated by what may be an apocryphal story about Schopenhauer, a German philosopher. He was called the "dismal philosopher" by many, perhaps because of his interest in India and the seemingly hopeless lot of the lower caste, perhaps because of his attitude toward women. He could see no earthly use for females save to propagate the race and it was an oversight of the creator to have not provided some other way. He apparently did not have many friends. He did have a dog named "Atwa," Hindi for soul. Schopenhauer lived a well regulated life. He rose in the morning, had breakfast, studied and wrote, had lunch, took a nap, and then a walk. He walked at the same time every afternoon, took the same course, and walked in the same fashion with his hands clasped behind his back, his gaze fixed on his toes. He looked neither right nor left and never up. Folks in the town grew accustomed to him and just stayed out of his way. As fate would have it, one afternoon when Schopenhauer was taking his walk, an officer from the German army was walking through the village. He walked in a quite different fashion, arms swinging, body erect, and his gaze fixed just a little above the horizon. Here they were at the same time on the same side of the street, and they collided. Both fell to the dusty ground. The air turned a bit blue from the officer's expletives as he quickly got to his feet and feverishly brushed the dust from his uniform. As Schopenhauer slowly got to his feet, the officer blurted out at this little man, "Who do you think you are and where do you think you are going?" Schopenhauer didn't so much as raise his eyes as he quietly said, "Thank you sir, for formulating the two most important questions of all humankind." He put his hands behind his back, fixed a gaze on his toes, and resumed his walk.

I think we can make good use of a little fix on those two questions when we deal with survival. I will deal with only one of the many helps and helpers that are necessary to personal and cosmic survival. It is well characterized by a stance or perspective — standing outside ourselves. The Screwtape Letters aptly describes the power of seeing ourselves from the outside as a sense of proportion known best in humour. This is the one helper I suggest! Who we think we are and where we think we are going necessitates standing outside ourselves as humans, not gods, but creators with the creator. Humour, so common in the Bible, may be one of our best means of survival of adversity, illness, war, disaster, success. It is an important key to wellness — physically, socially, spiritually. "Standing outside ourselves" is a right brain activity. It requires imagination. Imagination is probably the main source of humor.

Humour is an important proclamation (Kerygma) and one of the most useful tools for survival. Like any learned skill, it can be good or bad, healthy or harmful, positive or negative, creative or destructive, loving or hateful, life-giving or death-dealing. It is a significant part of perspective and it is common to Biblical literature and stories about God. There are a few books that deal specifically with the Bible and humour: *The Screwtape Letters, The Comic Vision, And God Created Laughter: The Bible as Divine Comedy*, and many others on humour and the human situation. Another useful source is just a look around creation: plants, animals, and insects, especially humans. The creative sense of humour is about all that can account for some things in creation.

Who do you think you are? Hard though it may be, it is more imperative than ever that we understand and develop a comic perspective on ourselves and our relationships to others. It is a major tragedy to lose the sense of comic about ourselves. "Only in so far as we learn to take our ideologies and beliefs less absolutely, our self images less seriously, do we have a chance of softening tragic extremes and tragic extremism. If nothing else, people who have a refined sense of humour about themselves are less inclined to kill one another. They may even be more disposed to love one another," wrote C. Hyers. Dr. Christian Hageseth, a psychiatrist friend of mine, wrote a book on laughter and advised readers to take themselves lightly because they are not the centre of the universe, nor its director. Someone else has that job and is qualified. To be able to laugh at oneself may be one of the most useful of all graces. Hageseth reminds his readers that humour is not the same as jokes. Some jokes may be humourous. Some observers think humour is partly genetic. Some say it is a means of grace. Most say humourous perspective can be learned.

When we look at humour development, we may see how humour can be learned. Hageseth uses the illustration of the baby's smile. A baby can start smiling in response to stimulation at seven to eight weeks. We don't get a baby to smile or laugh by telling a joke. We make noises, make faces, tickle the chin, etc. Smiling is believed to be the first response in the development of humour. Hageseth says it is the last to be lost in senescence.

The two main sources of humour in adults are perspective and behaviour. These go hand in hand. One contributes to the other and they rarely exist in isolation. Smiling is behaviour and that behaviour has an effect on the feeling. Expressing the feeling with a smile or laugh changes the feeling by enhancing it. We act — smile — on what we perceive — inside our own heads and what we perceive in the environment. We don't necessarily act on what is out there. We act on what we perceive. It follows then, that our behaviour — we are still talking about smiling and humour — often shapes our world — especially our inner world. The words we use don't just reveal something about feelings. The words we persistently use affect feelings. Humourous behaviour shapes perception. What we see, we learn. What we learn, we practice. What we practice, we become. That's the way it seems to work with humour.

I made a list of the kinds of things positive humour can contribute to survival:

Positive humour can:
- shift human consciousness to healing, love, peacemaking.
- trigger endorphin release and increase immune resources.
- trigger the "butterfly effect" in human relations.
- be a drop of sweetness in a bucket of water — all the water is affected.
- be a drop of color in a pail of clear water — all is changed.
- help do grief work.
- reduce anxiety.
- bring people together.
- enhance communication.
- help people accept new ideas.
- contribute to good health.

- contribute to wellness — Norman Cousins' *Anatomy of an Illness* describes the role humor played in his recovery from a serious illness.
- create new shapes and new colors of love.
- help manage dangerous and life-threatening situations. Note war-time humour
- be a wonderful way to express love.
- creep into every part of life. If I asked us all to be silent for 30 seconds, and for no one to think of an elephant, you know what would happen.
- become our best defense against stress, burnout, the blues, depression.

Positive humour is:
- good psychic medicine.
- good political medicine.
- like all gifts of grace, a guide to reality.

Positive humour helps us in the church. R. M. Brown has written that the church is like Noah's Ark. If it weren't for such a great storm outside, we couldn't stand the smell inside.

I think positive humour is mostly a right brain activity that has a role somewhat like the "stranger attracters" in Chaos Science. It can be and is used by the Holy Spirit. Positive humour can be built into a belief system. There is ample material for it in Biblical memory systems and the common life. In these days of "user pay" talk and "user pay" systems, positive humour is free. There may not be such a thing as a free lunch, but there is such a thing as positive, free humour.

In the wisdom of Ecclesiastes we are reminded that "for everything there is a season." Those who live in grace are freed from: the necessity of taking ourselves, our circumstances, our morality, our failures, our faith, too seriously. We are free to play and work, laugh and cry, as children of God. That's who we think we are. And where do we think we are going? Ours is a pilgrimage of faith, and faith is to be transparent. There is no proof for faith. The meaning is known in the process — in the journey. The quality, the virtue, the strength, the comfort, the peace and every other thing that comes on the journey has its season and all are meaningful enough to continue the journey of faith.

My wish for you all is to be "good humoured." We all need it. So to you all, "happy humourous faithing."

Children

*"Regardless of age, your child
never stops being your kid."*

Because our children arrived at four or five year intervals over a period of 14 years, Gretchen, the oldest, had ample opportunity to practice child care when she was young. These widely spaced children also meant that we had somebody at home for 33 years. Now that they are gone, I can see that children provide a dimension in family life that is no longer there when they leave. On a daily basis they force you to confront the generation that is to follow you. Regardless of age, your child never stops being your kid. You accept, even if you don't always agree with their judgment; you affirm them and rejoice in their abilities.

All four of our children learned early on how to cook, do their laundry, keep house and keep track of their money. I think participation was the key. They each received an allowance but it was contingent upon accomplishing certain basic chores such as making their beds and cleaning their room, doing their share of dishes, helping with yard work and completing homework.

Mark, the oldest of the three boys and the most independent, was the only one who never did his homework. He was smart enough that he could get away without doing it. He's the only one of the four who dropped out of college. After a stint in the Air Force, he settled into the world of work and today his income is the highest among my children. By the time he was 16, he'd earned enough money to buy and maintain his own car, a precedent both his younger brothers followed.

After a career of 28 years with Woodward Governor, Mark started his own Snap-On Tool business which he enjoyed except for the collection end of it. Eventually he quit and returned to the Governor system, working for a small company in New

Geller family en route to Sierra Leone, 1960.
Left to right: Mark, Gretchen, June, Vic, Tim

Orleans. When the company sold, he returned to Fort Collins for a time before he began consulting and doing special projects for a governor controls company in Florida. Today he lives with his wife and three step-daughters near Fort Lauderdale and manages the sales and service end of the business.

Mark still seeks my advice. When he has a decision to make, he often runs it by me, which I find quite interesting given his independent nature.

Gretchen and her husband, Butch, live in Butte, Montana with their daughter, Lew Yong. Gretchen, an RN, teaches medical technology online and in person. She's a graduate of Hastings College with a degree in math and for two years taught math and science in Ghana in the Peace Corps. In Pennsylvania, and in Wisconsin she was in community service and gardening.

When she decided to change careers, she took a year off and worked as a volunteer at Ghost Ranch in New Mexico before entering nursing school in Albuquerque. Gretchen is a person who speaks her mind and, like me, often asks the difficult questions. She found that she didn't always please the dean of the

Sunday best, 1965

nursing school, especially when she expressed her opinions about the subservient role nurses often played when interacting with doctors. There was no outright animosity but when Gretchen graduated number one in her class, no reference to this fact was to be found anywhere in the graduation program or during the ceremony.

During training she became interested in psychiatric nursing and found her first job working in the New Mexico state prison. Then she moved on to a job in a private adolescent treatment center in Albuquerque as director of nursing. When she moved to Montana with her husband, she worked first as a psych nurse in the state penitentiary and later as director of nursing in a state operated rehabilitation program for adolescents.

Eleven years ago Gretchen and Butch adopted Lew Yong who will soon be 14 and is a talented athlete and musician. The family lives in downtown Butte in a wonderful old restored home built in 1903. Butch is now chairman of the engineering department at Montana Technical University, part of the University of Montana system.

Young adults, 1975

At my eightieth birthday bash, my son Tim, gifted with language, was asked to say a few words: "Well," he started off, "my dad is not a saint, except in the Biblical sense where a saint is one who follows. He's not a saint in the Pauline sense, not in the ecclesiastical sense, and certainly not in the minds of the people who know him well. In fact, in college his nickname was 'Heller Geller.'"

Tim is a composer and businessman in Massachusetts. After working on a Ph.D in music at Princeton University, he switched gears and earned an MBA, which gave him the training he needed to create and operate a firm that specializes in alternative economic development, specifically building low cost housing and starting cottage industries. The work he does is a direct outgrowth of his masters' thesis in this field. "I wanted to see if I could get churches to support such a project — to put their money where their faith is," he told me. Today there are

The Geller family at Sutherland cabin, summer 2006.
Back row, left to right; Chris, Mark, Tim, Gretchen, Vic, Butch.
Front row: June, Lew Yong, Bob

many UCC (Congregational) churches, a synagogue and several Episcopal parishes participating. They lend money from their endowment funds at rates as low as one percent to the company that Tim created.

In his "other life" Tim composes classical and religious music for organs, string quartets, and bell choirs. He no longer plays the bassoon that made him so popular in New Zealand, but he often conducts performances of his own compositions. The symphony he wrote as part of his graduate work at Princeton earned him first place and $15,000 in an international composers' competition. The award, the Genestera Prize, is named after an Argentinean composer by that name. Tim's work has been performed in Spain, Portugal, the Canary Islands, New York, Boston, Cleveland and at Colorado State University. It pleases me that he used some of my poetry as part of one of his compositions.

Vic, our youngest, lives in Fort Collins, where he manages

the warehouse for ComCast, the latest incarnation in what has been Columbine Television, MCI and AT and T. He found his way to Columbine as an installer while he was in college and needed a summer job. After three years on a football scholarship at Hastings College, he dropped his scholarship to concentrate on drama, his first love. He has performed in musicals and plays in Fort Collins, but these days his job takes so many hours that he no longer has time for anything more than a few hours of fishing a week, and some hunting in the fall.

He does find the time to have lunch with June and me, sometimes as often as four times a week, and on Sundays he often cooks for us. It's very nice to have him around. I am especially grateful for his help with heavy lifting in the yard.

Bob with trademark bolo, 2007

Bolo Ties

"For as long as I can remember, I've fussed tying neckties."

From the time I was in seminary, I owned bolo ties and wore them, but only occasionally. Now and then I found an occasion to wear one when I was in West Virginia and in Arizona. For as long as I can remember, I've fussed about tying neckties. I wore clip-ons for a while after I discovered them, but found they fell off too easily. Bolos have saved me from ties. I probably have 40 of them. Many have been given to me and several are reminders of time spent in West Africa and in New Zealand. I especially treasure a bolo that belonged to longtime CSU president Bill Morgan, given to me by his daughter, Dorcas Murray, after he died.

Over the years, when I did something June didn't like, she'd often threaten me: "I'll have you laid out in a necktie." I miss June's sense of humor that has faded over time due to disease, pain and many medications.

Caregiver

"By caring for June, my love for her has taken on a new and enriching dimension."

I didn't have to interview for my third career. It came on slowly at first, then later full force. I had no prior training, so most of what I do, I learned on the job. I did have a choice, whether or not to accept this position, but in the end, I didn't think about it for long, and the decision was easy. The hours are long but the returns are great, and there's little chance I'll ever be fired.

June had her first surgery for arthritis in 1969 when her neck was operated on to relieve pain caused by a combination of osteo and rheumatoid arthritis, from which she has suffered for many years. That was the beginning of a series of surgeries that have included two back fusions, three knee replacements, and gall bladder and stomach surgery unrelated to arthritis.

In 2003 June's arthritis took a severe turn which landed her in the hospital for observation. The narcotics she had been taking for pain were no longer working and a new approach was needed. She was given a shot, which resulted in a few months of freedom from pain, but not before she spent nearly three weeks in a rehabilitation center recovering from the critical episode.

At the same time, the beginnings of dementia showed up, possibly because of oral medications that kept her in a daze, but also because of vascular constriction, although we can't be sure of the causes. She came home weak, on a catheter and unable to do much of her own personal care. At that time I spoke with her doctor about my wish to provide her care, if that were possible.

For the first few months, we had the assistance of certified nursing assistants who came twice a week, and a physical therapist who came weekly. When time ran out for the aides paid for by Medicare, I worked out a schedule which included some

Bob and June dressed for a costume party, 1941

assistance from aides I hired myself and a nurse who came every two weeks to change June's catheter.

After six months, I suggested to June's doctor that we try to get rid of the catheter. The process was long and slow and required bladder retraining, but was accomplished by February 2004, freeing us up to go more places and even spend time in the mountains that summer with our children.

About this time I discovered a helpful text on caregiving called *The Thirty-Six-Hour Day*, which discusses dementia as well as the demands of on-going personal care for a loved one. June was still taking an array of oral medications that left her in a daze much of the time. She could not take medications by

June and Bob, 63rd wedding aniversary, December 10, 2007

herself, and needed help with eating her meals. Again, I asked her doctor about the possibility of cutting back on medications, and he agreed. One at a time, we eliminated three prescriptions with the result that she became more alert and capable of caring for herself. Fortunately, the pain they were designed to address did not return.

Near the end of 2004, June and I were sitting together in the dining room. I was writing checks, and without any warning, she suddenly fell from her chair and broke her collarbone. Despite the pain, she was able to stay off the medications during this time. After a stay in the hospital, she moved to a rehabilitation center where she had to re-learn how to use a walker with only one arm for support. During the following months, she was able to give up another three medications that she had been taking for a long time without any ill effects.

Now she takes six pills most days as opposed to the eleven she'd been taking in the past. At home she spends most of her time in a wheelchair, but she is able to use a walker for a few steps. She's faithful about her physical therapy and has far fewer times when she is confused. They often occur at the end of a long day or for a short time early in the morning. She no longer drives, but still enjoys shopping trips and choosing her own clothes, though it takes her a very long time to make a decision. While she is unable to dress without help, she can put on her own make-up, and that's probably a good thing!

The nights are easier than they once were. There was a time when I got up three, sometimes four, times a night to help her to the bathroom. Now it is usually only twice. I set an alarm and then awaken her. We rarely have an accident now. I've learned to help June in the shower and to do personal care so well that one doctor told me June was probably the cleanest lady in town.

Paid aides and volunteers help out each week, giving me several hours at a time when I can work, shop, and do errands. On Wednesdays June's friend and aide, Phyllis, makes lunch, our main meal of the day. On Fridays an aide arrives at 6 a.m. so that I can be at the Friday Morning Book Group by 7 a.m. On Sundays, our son Vic makes lunch.

I've learned that June cannot be left alone, for fear that she will doze, wake up, and try to get up and search for me. I can work in the yard for short periods, and check on her frequently, and I can work in another room when she is resting. My neighbor will help out in a pinch if I need to pick up groceries or medications.

Our routine is firmly set, the same every week. There have been times when the schedule has been wearing for me, but a strange thing has happened over time. The chores that were once wearisome have become things I want to do for her. For all the years that I worked two jobs and was heavily involved with the Presbytery as well, I depended on June too much to run the house, take care of the children, and pay the bills. I did make breakfast while June got everyone ready for school, but other than that, I had no household duties. Today I do all the grocery shopping and all the cooking except for the few meals each week that others prepare for us.

While most of the time the duties I've taken on are not a burden, it doesn't mean that it is always easy. One of the things I find difficult is when I think I'm going to have a block of time to complete a task, it is often interrupted by an immediate need of June's. It's not unlike life with a small child.

It has been difficult for June to become the recipient instead of the giver of care. Even though she does what she can — folding clothes, putting silverware away, and helping with cookie making — she's aware of the huge change in her role, and sometimes expresses her feelings with words like, "I'm not worth anything any more." I've found that it is important to address these feelings as soon as she expresses them, and to emphasize to her my appreciation for the things she is able to do. If not, the moment is gone, and she may not remember it later.

Even during her worst periods, music has been a comfort for June. When she attends a concert, or even when she watches an especially good music program on television, something snaps in her and there is clarity. Her enjoyment is obvious and afterwards she's able to discuss the music in detail. This is particularly true for choral music, her specialty. We still attend the symphony and the Larimer Chorale, and for many summers looked forward to the opera in Fort Collins. Plays have become more of a problem because it is difficult for her to follow the dialogue.

June delights in flowers and in the summer months we often have an early supper and go over to the CSU gardens on Lake Street to wander up and down the aisles identifying and talking about the different plants. It is a pleasure for both of us.

Would I trade my current career? Never. It has surprised me by taking our relationship to a deeper level. By caring for June, my love for her has taken on a new and enriching dimension.

Providing a high level of care for a spouse is not the norm; it is not what most men expect to do. For so many years, we didn't have time to take care of each other. Now I do, and June, to the extent of her ability, does too.

Coincidence?

"I've given a great deal of thought to the reasons why my life has taken the turns it has and why."

My mother always said I was born with a question mark in my head. It may be true. I've been asking questions all my life. I ask questions because I'm curious — I want to know the why of things — and I want to know how things work. Being able to question is important to me.

These days I wonder less than I used to, or maybe it's just that I no longer feel such a strong need to have all my questions answered. Keeping an open mind and being able to question is often more important than finding an answer. When one no longer feels the need to question, growth and learning end.

I've given a great deal of thought to the reasons why my life has taken the turns it has and why. So many things have happened to me that could have been coincidences, or could have come about through divine guidance. Perhaps it has been some of both. I don't know and I'm not sure who to ask. What I do know is that regardless of the reasons, I am thankful. It makes sense to be thankful. In fact it may be true that gratitude is essential for all of us.

I have asked myself why I wasn't born in a slum in India to a drunken mother. I have found no reason why. But still, I can be thankful for when and where I was born, and for the family that nurtured me.

Why, I have asked myself, did Kenneth Reeves, an extremely bright person, come to the tiny town of Dalton, Nebraska as a seminary student, and why did he decide to stay? If he hadn't been my mentor during high school, I might never have decided to become a minister.

Why, when I was only 14, did I drive the family car into

Bob and June celebrate 50 years of marriage, December 10, 1994

town every week to choir practice? I don't know, but if it hadn't been for that experience, I would never have learned how to read music, a skill that I have appreciated all my life.

Why did I decide to become a Boy Scout? Why does anyone? Why was I chosen to go to the Boy Scout World Jamboree in Washington DC? Without that experience I would not have developed the wider view of the world given me by that trip and my association with boys from all over the world.

Why did I get a scholarship to Hastings College? I know, I came in second in my graduating class, and that helped, but why did they choose me? And why did the Presbyterian Church decide to take me "under care" when I was only 16? This gave me ministerial status and an exemption from the service when I signed up for the draft at age 18.

Why, on the second Sunday in November 1940, was I recruited to be part of a "gospel team" from Hasting College, to preach in a small Nebraska town? And why, on that team, were there two women singers, one of them June, who would later become my wife? She was a freshman and I a junior and after the service we gave, she invited our team to her home in Grand Island. A crazy thought ran through my head when I met her beautiful white-haired grandmother, and her mother, whose hair was beginning to turn the same lovely color. "Maybe I should find myself a woman like this," I said to myself.

Not long afterwards, I began walking June home to her dormitory from the library, and now and then sharing 10-cent doughnuts and coffee with her at the small cafe across the street from the library. And soon we were double-dating with my roommate and his girlfriend....

Why did I decide to join the debate and extemporaneous speaking teams in college? Maybe because I liked to talk. But without that experience, I would not have sharpened my listening skills to the point where I could pick up on an opponent's weakness and be able to use it to make a point of my own.

And why, after seminary, did I decide to go to the Labor Temple in New York City and become part of the controversial industrial ministry of the Presbyterian church? If I hadn't, I would never have known the director of the program where I served in West Virginia and would never have learned his four rules for orienting a life:

1. Plant a tree (This gets you down on your knees).
2. Rear a child.
3. Write a book.
4. Celebrate.

I had so many choices in seminary, why did I pick the field work I did, from serving in Utah, to counseling in a mental hospital, to pastoring in a rural parish? Why did I choose student work in a wealthy suburban church, in a settlement house, at West Madison Street Mission, and Salvation Army "pick up" of drunks passed out on Chicago streets?

Was it pure luck that landed me in West Africa? Why did the request to fill a position there come to me, and why, with four small children, did I decide to take it?

Why, when I applied for a Danforth grant to study psychiatry and religion, was I chosen from among many?

Why, a few weeks ago when I mentioned to a friend my hope to be able to go to New Zealand one more time, contingent upon a healthy income tax return, did I discover, a couple of weeks later, two airline tickets with June's and my name on them? Luck? Good fortune? Coincidence? Divine intervention?

I wonder, but beyond wondering, I give thanks. I accept what I've been given with a gratitude that, as much as I am able, takes the form of giving something in return. Gratitude is essential to understanding life.

Poetry Over the Years

"I go to poetry out of memory..."

I've always enjoyed writing poetry, for special occasions and to record insights and incidents that have been important to me. Many were written on small scraps of paper, and many were given away, and I kept no copy. I really don't know very much about poetry and I don't actually understand why it is that I write some poetry but mostly doggerel. It mostly just "happens" in my head and I write it down. No matter. They belong to the world.

I like poetry for many reasons, but there has been one pleasure that I had not expected. Every year since I started writing a poem in our Christmas letter, I have received written comments, most often like this: "I look forward to your Christmas letter every year for a poem. I have saved most of them."

There have been a few poems that I have written to a special friend after a loss in his or her life or just to describe something I have observed in a person's life. Here are two illustrations.

In 1991–92 we lived in Otaki, New Zealand where I was a volunteer in a parish. The couple who owned the house where we lived became close friends. Harry was very active in the parish and I noticed his style of churchmanship and community service. It taught me much when I was 70 years old. I put his style of life in a little four-line piece of doggerel in February 1992:

Many people are good at talking about what they are doing, but in fact, do little.
Others do a lot but don't talk about it.
They are the ones who make and sustain community.

The last time we visited New Zealand in 2007, Harry was at a church dinner and like many others, he took some time to be at our table. In the course of our conversation he pulled a slip of paper out of his billfold and asked, "Do you remember this?"

I said, "I do now, after reading it,"

"I think I have read this over a thousand times since you gave it to me," Harry said. It had been more than 15 years.

Two weeks later, Harry, who was 90 years old, had a massive heart attack and died. His daughter went through his billfold, found the poem and put it in the folder prepared for his memorial service.

Another example is related to a poem I wrote for a good friend in Fort Collins when he lost his wife in 1991. I was in New Zealand. I have given the poem to several friends after the death of a spouse or close family member. Some have told me afterwards that it seemed to mean the most to them when they read it aloud to themselves. The poem is in the resources that Hospice shares in some circumstances. It's called *Remembrance.*

Remembrance

I come to this holy place
and stand
alone
and wonder —
a place anointed,
set apart
because you were here.

Wistful memories
and friendly ghosts
hover on the edges
of my mind
and I remember
what this place
was like
when you were here.

You have gone
and I am alone.
Your life has taken on
A dimension I can only imagine.
But what we shared is no less
just because you are not here.

Shadows replace sunlight,
echoes replace laughter,
reflected images replace
sights of happy days.

Indelibly stamped
permanently etched,
forever preserved,
are the memories of you
and this special place,

in a hidden
corner of my heart.

For blessed memories
Oh Lord,
I thank you.

Revised, February, 1994

I go to poetry out of memory and it seems that when I remember, I go to poetry — perhaps everyone does — so that we might more fully inhabit our lives and the world in which we live them. If we more fully inhabit our lives and our world, we may be less likely to destroy either of them. The pieces that follow are a selection of my poetry written between 1944 and 2006.

Chicago

Long night of dusty shadows,
Slow tread of workers' feet,
Heads hung low when passing
the cold and barren street.

No bed for weary workers,
No roof above their head —
While hunger stalks the alleys
Beside the living dead.

All night I hear the tramping
Of weary workers' feet
Groping through the darkness
And stumbling down the street.

Written after spending a weekend in West Madison Street Mission in the winter of 1943–1944. Christmas Eve.

Lament

If I have wept, beloved, forgive my tears.
Had I but loved you less, I had wept more,
And darkened the bright stars, and stilled the song
Of mockingbird at night, and larks at dawn
And beat my heart against the hidden door.

O bitter night that catches at my breath
What is this paradox of life and death
That wells within me now that love is gone
Beyond all sight and touch, but nearer still
Than this soft wind that touches on the hill
Than this hushed morning of woodland song.

Oh yet, forgive me if I weep anon
To see the moon arise so thin and new
To see the stars look down in vain for you
To hear the night bird with his plaintiff song.

From green to sear the spring to summer yields;
How can I look upon these fading fields
Where small green fragments of the spring remain
In sheltered spots along the northern slopes
And not despair of all our shattered hopes.
Of all we loved, how little is the same.

alternative last verse

From brown to green the winter to spring yields;
How can I look upon these lively fields
Where small brown fragments of the winter remains
Snow in sheltered spots along the northern mountain
slopes
And not despair of all our shattered hopes —
Of all we loved, how little is the same.

1988

Today and Tomorrow

I Will Live Today and Tomorrow
...and each day coming as if this were the beginning
of my own very special life.
Life still holds joys and surprises for me.
There will still be surprises and sunsets...
Children's little hands that need holding...
Friends to laugh with and to comfort...
Flowers to tend...
and weeds to pull!!
Cookies to bake...
and to eat!
Fresh coffee,
Hugs.
So...
grieve your losses,
shed your tears.
Then...
Live life fully...
enjoy all its richness...
And rejoin us on this incredible, beautiful path of life.

Best wishes. Bob Geller for the MDH Hospice,
Macomb, Illinois.
1988–1989

To Those I Love

Whenever I leave you whom I love,
to go along the silent way,
Grieve not, nor speak of me with tears,
but laugh and talk of me as if I were
beside you there.
I'd come, I'd come, could I but find a way,
but would not tears and grief be barriers?
So when you hear a song or see a bird I loved,
please do not let the thought of me be sad,
for I am loving you just as I always have.
You were so good to me.
There are so many things I wanted still to do,
so many things I wanted to say to you.
Remember that I did not really fear,
It was just leaving you that was so hard to face.
We cannot see beyond, but this I know:
I loved you so, t'was heaven here with you.

Jo Abrams memorial
September 1989

I adapt this poem for individual use for a memorial
service.

For 100 Seasons
For 25 years
For Love, Peace, Joy,
Dedication, Forgiveness, Faith, Hope, Patience.
Rejoice.
And give thanks
To the Lord.

1991

Go Forth

I like "sending forth" better than "benediction" because, in most people's minds, benediction means, "that's it folks." This "Go Forth" is informed by American Indian spirituality, Jewish/Christian spirituality, Aborigine spirituality, and Maori spirituality.

Walk *care-fully* as you go
from here.
The Spirit is there before you.
Walk humbly as you go from
here.
The World awaits your coming.
Walk softly as you go
from here,
For the Spirit is abroad in all the earth
And the voice of the Spirit
speaks in every time and place.
Go simply, lightly, gently in faith and
may the Shalom of God — Peace go
With us all.
So be it — Amen

1992

The Work of Christmas

When the song of the angels is stilled,
When the star in the sky is gone,
When the kings and princes are home, when the
shepherds are back with their flock,
The work of Christmas begins —

to find the lost,
to heal the broken,
to feed the hungry,
to release the prisoners,
to rebuild the nations,
to bring peace among sisters and brothers,
to make music in the heart.

1993

When Lent Comes

You have to put away the tinsel,
You have to take down the Christmas tree,
and stand out in the open...vulnerable.
You either are or you aren't.
You either believe or you won't.
And, oh Lord, how we love the stable and the star!
When Lent comes, the angel voices
begin their lamenting,
And we find ourselves in a courtyard
where we must answer
Whether we know him or not.

*Holiday Inn, Honolulu Airport 1993, on the way home
from New Zealand.*

God's World

There aren't many things in life that we are sure of —
but one:
Everything must change.
The young must become old,
and the old must die.
Change is certain.
A fact that holds our days together
and shapes our tomorrows.
We all know that
rain must fall
snow must melt
and clouds must scatter.

Oh, how glad I am that
God doesn't change!

God is forever constant,
Fulfilling promises and giving love.
Alleluia!

May 3, 1993
Written at Woodward Governor, Fort Collins,
after a counseling session.

For June

When I think
of how my life
would have been
without you,
I see little!
Because you
have helped me
become me.
You have opened my eyes
to a new life;
leaving others is
easy when
I am loved.

June 14, 1993

Friends and Friendship

As I sit lazily under the old pine tree, I cast my eyes on the
beauty around me:
Autumn sunlight slanting through a hazy afternoon;
The last birds feeding hungry mouths...it's bedtime soon;

The golden-toasted leaves awaiting a signal to fall,
As soon old man winter will make his next call;

The cool autumn breeze playing tag with the dandelion;
All the remaining birds communicating...oh, so many kinds;

The deer sunbathing; the tall weeds holding hands;
A butterfly trapped in a cocoon, making his next plans;

From the back patio a tourist train whistle fills the air;
The gray squirrel busily hides peanuts without much care.

Thank you, God, for blessing me with these things.
Help me appreciate them. Let my heart sing.
Later this afternoon it rained — nearly everything looked different.

September, 1993.

Christmas 1993

Already another year is nearly over —
Measure not your spirit's worth
by summing up your years.

Our Journey in Life

Come along with me
as a sojourner in faith.
Bring along
a sense of expectancy,
a vision of high hopes,
a glimpse of future possibility,
a vivid imagination
For God's creation is not done.

Let us travel light
In the spirit of faith and expectation
Toward the God of our hopes and dreams.
May we be witnesses
to God's future breaking in.
Come along with me
as sojourners in faith
secure in the knowledge
that we never travel alone.

1994

The Church

We are like common pots...the supreme power belongs to God.   *— 2 Corinthians 4: 7*

The Church is like a common pot.
It can be used —
to feed the hungry,
to carry water to the thirsty,
to hold God's created nature,
to display the beauty of our Creator.

The Church is like a common pot.
It is fragile —
easily broken,
often set aside or lost,
sometimes crushed.

The Church is like a common pot.
It is dependent upon the skill of the Potter;
it is His image in clay;
it must yield to His touch.

The Church is like a common clay pot.
It has purpose;
its beginning was in our Creator's mind;
its existence is within its bounds.

Yet,
unlike a common clay pot
the Church
has life,
has free will;
it can be more than it is
when it prays and sings —
"Have thine own way, Lord, have thine own way.
Thou art the Potter, I am the clay."

October 1994

For 200 Seasons—
For 50 Years

For Love, Peace, Joy,
Dedication, Forgiveness,
Faith, Hope, Patience.
Rejoice and
Give thanks
to the Lord.

1995

We Will Never See This Day Again—

The seconds nor the hour.
Now's the time to take the time
To stop and smell the flowers.
Today's the day to give a smile
And happiness away
That you were saving for a friend
Some rainy, gloomy day.
This day is golden, priceless.
God made this day for you.
The deed you do for someone else
May just come back to you.
So touch a heart; hold a hand;
And call that lonely friend.
Don't postpone the love you have.
This day won't come again.

February 1995

Winter's Art

Winter is a poet who,
in quiet meditation,
writes of mountains blanketed
by white precipitation.

Winter is an artist, too,
and softly draws the scene
of stillness in a frozen pond
against a silent screen.

Winter is a musician,
and if we're listening,
the grace-note of God's love is played
which no one's voice can sing.

September 1997

A world without God is like
an idea without a mind;
or, a flower without sun;
or, a family without parents;
or, a poem without meaning;
or, a love without a lover;
or, a soul without a body;
a person without a purpose
is like a world without God
a hidden world...

March 27, 1998

A House Blessing

God bless the corners of this house,
And be the lintel blest;
And bless the hearth and bless the board;
And bless each place of rest;
And bless each door that opens wide,
For stranger as to kin;
And bless each crystal window pane
that lets the starlight in;
And bless the rooftree overhead
And every sturdy wall;
The peace of man, the peace of God,
the peace of love on all.

1998
Ludwig Cabin

'Tis Spring

So let us sing
Of things to See
And things to Be
Like Purple Blossoms on the Tree
And Nectar for the Honey Bee
And
Love and Loving for
You and me.

March 2002

To Love: A Plea

Love,
look me
in the deep-blue-black pupil
of my eye.
Face me.
Don't turn away like a thief
who has stolen
my treasures.

I gave you my heart.
You didn't steal it,
So, Love, stay.

Watch over me
like a good shepherd
who watches with and over his flock;

And,
who walks softly in the green pastures
where the grass rises
to lend a gentle voice to the winds.

Skip with me
through the desolate
and perpendicular November rain
where the mud puddles
are made from the pains
of past Octobers.

Go with me
through the revolving doors
of boredom,
then
touch my heart with a drama
that befits my imagination.

Help me
to dream of old things
while reaching for new worlds
beyond my own and my known.

Love,
spread over and stir me
like the pink-palmed down,
in early morning
spreads over the quiet and sleeping city
to stir slumberers awake.

Go with me through all my day.
Sit with me at the midday hour,
and
intensify my longings
as the Sun's light
is intensified
when it reaches the noon-height.

Climb with me
to the big-and-holy towers
where we may sit on laughing rooftops
and look below at blind men
who march in grim formation
over the rubble of their own loneliness.

Love,
please abide with me.
Quieten my heart-ache fears.
Travel with me
through my hours
and through my seasons.
Be as close to me
as frost on an iced glass.

And Love,
between my dusk
and my dawn,
Sleep with me...
Sleep with me...
Sleep with me
through a thousand
births, deaths, and rebirths,
then
rise with me
in the rain-bowed beauty
of my ultimate resurrection.

2003

Time

Time ticks by and memories are made.
The young wait eagerly for time to pass,
yet the old folks pray for time delayed
that they might stop the hourglass.

The clock may stop, but time moves on.
Too much time is wasted.
The years go by and are gone
with joys we've never stated.

Time is measured by the sun,
making magic in the sky.
We cannot capture any day
no matter how we try.

The love we've shared with others
and accomplishments we've made
are moments and the memories
that time will never fade.

December 31, 2004

The Secret Kiss

At the heart of the universe
is
a secret
around which
the
ebb and flow
of
all existence
circles
as a dog
circles
for
a safe place to lie down.

In the heart of each one of us
is
the answer
around which
the
ebb and flow
of
our lives
circles
as a hummingbird.
This
is the
nectared flower
inside
the Kiss
that
melts
secrets
and *answer*
into one.

Make the World Beautiful

I see war and death
and ask, "Where is God?"
I see poverty, ghettos and
 hunger.
I see hypocrisy, anger and
starvation.
I see hatred and discrimination.
I see abuse of children and women.
 and I ask, "Where is God?"
Then I think about the Creator
giving us freedom to follow.
It is our decision to work with
Her or Him.
In love and understanding,
And then I ask, "Where are
the people?"
Stand Up, and help make the
world beautiful.
Let's go!

December 2005

"I Am 85 Years Old"

I am a collection of all my years,
Enriched with
Your life stories,
Your glories,
Your troubles,
Your tears.
Tales of your lifetimes
Live in my eyes.
So I am 85 years wise.

You are my connections
To far away places
That live in my thoughts
Of good times and dear
faces.
Your histories shine in me
and
Fill me with light.
I am 85 years old,
And wise.

We think we know just who we are
And what we can or cannot do.
And then God puts someone
in our lives
Who shows us potentials we've never
Touched or even imagined.
Will life never stop amazing me?

2006

Friend

My friend, soon you will into retirement be going.
But in a way, you're not really going.
Part of you will always stay with me here.
That's the way it is with friendships dear.

My friend, we've shared so many good times —
Learning to harmonize, making up rhymes.
Together we've sung; we've laughed; talked;
and prayed.
Memories of moments that won't ever fade.

My friend, you've helped me much more than you
know.
I'm still learning to trust, to risk, and to grow.
I treasure the friendship you've given me.
Just remember that you're very special to me.

undated
Jim White's retirement

Age

The mind grows young,
Wise and wonderful.
The body grows old,
Stiff and wrinkled.
Beauty fades
And only personality is left.
We call them old
And frail.
Not youth, old folks, but you may be the
hope of tomorrow,
For you, old folks, have the wisdom of yesterday.

undated

Come —
Sing to me.
Sing to me of life, of love, of laughter.
But don't sing *at* me —
Sing in to my heart!
Then I can experience
that life of friendship
that life of love
the love humane
that life of laughter
the life of laughter of God's children.

undated

So closely
You held my soul
that your roses filled it with
golden fragrance,
giving me life and warmth.
So long
the tie between us
that I can blossom towards
infinity, and never be
hindered
by your sheltering branches.

So joyous
the dance you taught me
that I have learned to
run and laugh in
innocence;
to really see the stars.

So bright
the sunshine you spilled in my heart
that the music flows richly
and evenly,
melting obstacles and worries
in love.

So closely —
So long —
So joyous —
So bright.

undated
Confidante, New Zealand

At
this winter's
turning
of the year
let us go gently
— for once —
into the night,
its dream-drenched,
glittering stillness
a haven for our souls.

There
is something
beyond the dull
brightness of midday,
florescent and buzzing.
Something to praise
beyond the sun,
triumphing over the intricacies
of shadowed moonlight.

January 18, 2008

A Sending Forth

The piece below is perhaps the most often used of all my poetry.
I often close events at which I speak with these words:

Go in love, keep your faith,
Give your faith away.
Work hard, play enough,
Laugh often, make peace,
And hang loose.
So be it. Amen and Amen

1970

Appendix

The Work of
United Campus Ministry
(now The Geller Center
for Spiritual Development)

"I had a strong conviction that the CSU students who made their homes in Fort Collins for four years or more, ought to become involved in their community."

A plaque attached to the east wall of the Geller Center reads:

Robert A. Geller
for
United Campus Ministry

The Geller House is dedicated to a vision of ministry with students, faculty, and staff of Colorado State University that seeks justice and the truth; honors others; affirms the uniqueness of each person and challenges people to claim their own faith.

June 24, 1990

When I received the Human Relations Award from the City of Fort Collins for the work I had done to encourage the establishment of nonprofit groups and to nurture their growth into independent organizations, I was asked to say a few words. Not one to miss an opportunity, I said that I was honored to receive this award but I'd noticed that over the years, it had never been given to a woman. I suggested that the committee might perhaps be a little behind the times. Hadn't they noticed that often women made more contributions to human relations than men did? After that, some women were presented with the Human Relations Award, and, on at least one occasion, a man and woman were chosen to share the award. I like to think that my attempt at consciousness-raising made an impression.

When I came to Fort Collins in 1962, I made it a priority to get to know not only the movers and shakers at the university, but also the people who held positions of power in the community. I took note of neighborhoods like Spanish Colony, now Alta Vista, Buckingham, and Andersonville, with unpaved streets and no running water. I walked the streets and alleys and struck up conversations with everyone I saw who could speak English.

I had a strong conviction that the CSU students who made their homes in Fort Collins for four years or more ought to become involved in their community. From small beginnings and with the help of many like-minded people, things began to happen. In the past 45 years, the programs that developed have been both affirming, and in some instances, controversial. No fewer than three CSU presidents "carefully" characterized the UCM in such terms as: "The UCM may well be the most relevant, progressive, respected, and trusted ministry to higher education at CSU." Several deans have joined those presidents, and two former Fort Collins mayors, Ms. Nancy Gray and Ms. Ann Azari, have shared observations of UCM. Nancy Gray said in a public meeting, "I can hardly believe how much a campus ministry has contributed to our city in kinds of services it has started or resources it has provided to community folks developing services that meet important human needs."

Did you ever know? Hardly anyone knows and even fewer remember, the origins of some of these important services. Some have come and gone but many still exist that have "spun off" to fund themselves. Several are now partially funded through the United Way. This "spin-off" was always a part of the philosophy of UCM: If a service demonstrated its relevance, it should spin off on its own at CSU and in Fort Collins.

The underlying philosophy of the UCM staff has been to develop resources in the community that students could use or volunteer in. These resources were to help them experience involvement in Fort Collins and offer them a good deal more than working in city food services and other jobs for pay.

The university is not an "island" in the city. It is the students' community while they are at the university, and it helps students mature as citizens to be involved in "service" in productive ways.

The central concept of ministry at CSU has been to help make a better learning community, one that includes the essential spiritual component of the whole person.

With time, the list of nonprofit organizations that got their start through UCM grew long. Below is a list and short histories that were included in the program for a fund-raising gala for the Geller Center in honor of my 85th birthday. The services that continue today are starred.

Colorado State University Community
*Black Student Services
*Fellowship of Christian Athletes
*Medical services for students, spouses, children
*First Day Care Center in married student housing
*International Students House
*Student Alcoholics Anonymous
*Student Al-Anon
*Student Crisis Hotline
*Listening Post, now "Talk to a Pastor"
*Senior Students Art Exhibit

*CSU credit for field work in Fort Collins (for more than journalism majors)
Tutoring for Junior High students
Meeting place for new student groups — Welsh Society, Young Republicans, Young Democrats, Jews for Jesus
*Campus Crusade for Christ
*Alternative Spring Break activities
Hillel Student Housing
Theology Day on campus
*Luncheon discussion for graduate students and older learners
*Friday Morning Book Group
Lazarus Tomb Coffee House
*Twelve Step Group for sexually addicted men
*Recruitment for full-time clergy
*Seminary Intern Training
Teaching Art Exhibits
Religion in Life Week
*Friends (Quakers) Meeting
Community Service (court requirements)
*Holocaust Week
*International Student Center
*Recruitment of full-time religious workers
*Agape Dinners
*Danforth Chapel weekly meditation
*Weekend retreats for learning and fellowship
*Hillel Ministry at CSU for Jewish Students
*Hartshorn Health/Day Services (student choice: rehab or dismissal)

Fort Collins Community
*Women's Crisis Center (Women's Center)
*Volunteer Clearing House (Education and Life Training Center)
Buckingham Neighborhood House
Viva House, Andersonville

The Point Drug and Alcohol Center
*Fort Collins Interfaith Council
*Peace and Justice Center
*Religious Movement Resource Center for Dangerous Cults
   and Hate Groups
*Downtown Food Bank
Community Service for offenders
Draft Information Center
Twelve Step Movement for Gambling and Sexual Addiction
*Buckingham Park
*Location for peace demonstrations to meet before marching
   to Old Town

The Women's Crisis Center

The Women's Crisis Center was organized and for its first two-and-a-half years it was officed in the Campus Ministry. Martha Bartholomew and several other women, along with Campus Ministry staff, organized the plan. The services were handled mostly through telephone and personal interviews. Trained listeners handled the "call-in line" and interviews. Referrals were usually made to agencies and some churches in Fort Collins, Estes Park, and Loveland before those cities developed their own services. Later the Crisis Center was divided into The Women's Center and the Community Crisis Hot Line. Both services exist today.

Volunteer Clearing House

VCH was organized in 1964 and based in UCM for three years. Developed by Fran Thompson, Marcielle Wood and UCM staff, it grew rapidly and had two other sites before moving to 401 Linden St. The building had been a lard rendering plant and required major clean up and painting. VCH first provided information for people interested in volunteering in existing nongovernmental community services. It soon developed classes in sewing, cooking, canning, teaching English, and tutoring.

VCH started Caravan to help those without transportation get to medical and other appointments. It later became city-operated Dial-a-Ride. After 15 years, VCH was renamed Education and Life Training Center. It has four divisions: administration, volunteer network, adult and literacy classes, and back to school bags for low-income children. It is now funded by United Way and has its own annual fund drive.

Fort Collins Area Interfaith Council

The Interfaith Council replaced the Fort Collins Council of Churches and was organized by Rev. John Minear of Laporte, director of Catholic Services Northern and the UCM staff in the basement of UCM. Part of its genius was the absence of a creedal statement of faith as a requirement for membership by local churches. Membership size determined dues. Churches could opt to participate in whatever community services or lobbying in state government they chose, and they were free to not participate in ways that didn't fit the mission and style of their church. At two monthly meetings one is devoted to reports from community services the council shares in and any developing need, and the other is for business. It is the most relevant interfaith council I have seen in 60 years. The council helped with establishment of the Fort Collins Children's Clinic, often referred to as the "Free Clinic."

Viva House, Andersonville

In 1964 Marcielle Wood donated a small house with a detached garage in Andersonville to UCM. The buildings were renovated, sewer and septic tank cleaned out, and water from the well piped into the house. Professor David Pettus, CSU, Waldo Young, a local builder, and Rev. Jim White, leader of a student team, refurbished nearly all of the kitchen and dining niche. Barb and Les Fraley did most of the site clean-up and septic system. Several faculty members shared in the renovations. The garage was used as an activity room and the house was lived in by two students who conducted an after school program for elementary children and supervised a lending library and give-away with duplicate books from the city library. This service continued until 1971 when a former student began living in the house and did calling in Andersonville, helping residents to become annexed to the city, get city water, and modernize homes. In 1974 the house was broken into and the inside destroyed beyond repair. In 1975 the buildings were razed, the site sold to the city and the lot is now a "pocket park" with play equipment. Viva House Ministry served a much-needed children's service in the 60's and 70's.

Buckingham House

Marcielle Wood owned this house as a rental and in 1970 converted it to offices for a social ministry and housing counseling for the neighborhood. Some forward thinking on the part of UCM's Community Outreach Task Group to Poor Neighborhoods also supported the project. For one year it was the office of the Volunteer Clearing House. Its most significant contribution was the birthing of the Neighbor-to-Neighbor Ministry that exists as one of the best counseling services for low cost housing and temporary help for people who have difficulty paying rent. It has received some sizable grants that have improved the house and erected new homes for people in the area. Buckingham House was sold to a family in the immediate community for a home.

The Point

The Point developed in the basement of UCM as a ministry for drug and alcohol counseling. After only a few months, The Point acquired a large federal grant written by a professor in the Counseling Department at CSU. The grant enabled The Point to rent the large AAUW home on Mulberry Street for female students at CSU. The Point developed an extensive program of counseling and group therapy for students and others who had drug and alcohol problems using volunteer professionals for most services. The building also served many "drop ins" as well as developing a small service for free medical treatment for young children two nights a week. The grant ran out in five years and a skeleton staff of three returned to the renovated portion of the UCM basement and operated for two more years. Eventually the need for a service like The Point was largely absorbed by existing services in the community.

Draft Information and Counseling Center

This service was developed in 1968 by faculty members and some clergy and was housed in an office in the UCM house. It continued until the federal draft was discontinued in 1975. It served students at CSU and young men in the community who had to register for the draft, providing legal information about registration. It was very careful and vigilant about keeping within the law. However, it was learned in the 1970's from a former student who had gone into the U.S. Air Force that the FBI had taped the telephone line. The service never did a single thing that was not within the law. The FBI denied the taping until they were threatened with making the information public. This service to hundreds of young men provoked considerable hate mail and threatening phone messages to the Gellers. It was also the reason several area churches withdrew financial support of UCM.

Friends Meeting — Quakers

UCM was the Sunday morning meeting palace for the Fort Collins Friends Meeting from the early 60's until 1992 when the meeting acquired a home of its own on Vine Street. Many of the Quakers did volunteer work in the UCM office and on the property and helped supervise some of the men doing community service as part of their sentence.

Student AA and Alanon Groups

The first student AA and Alanon groups were started by UCM and were housed in the Center from 1986–1993 when they moved to the Student Health Center on CSU campus.

12-Step Group Therapy

UCM started the first 12-step program in Fort Collins for sexually addicted persons. It met at the UCM house from 1987–90 when it moved to the Larimer County Center for Mental Health facility. This groups tends to "come and go" with the interest and needs that emerge. It has always provided its own leadership patterned after AA.

Theology Day on Campus

UCM started a Saturday contemporary Hebrew-Christian Theology lecture and discussion at the UCM house and the Danforth Chapel. Speakers came from faculties of CSU, Iliff School of Theology and Denver University. This day continued from the early 70's until 1989.

Holocaust Week

Before there was a synagogue in Fort Collins or a Hillel program for Jewish students, UCM organized the first three years of Holocaust Observance, beginning in 1964. The centerpiece for this early observance was a black and white photo exhibit of 40 poster-size pictures of Holocaust scenes taken of concentration camps in Germany and Poland. This exhibit was displayed for a week each year in the CSU Student Center and then offered to local churches for display for the remainder of February 1964–67. UCM also arranged to have a professor from CSU lead a discussion of the Holocaust in the Student Center. This has become a powerful educational tool at CSU, with a week of events and speakers organized by the Hillel group and Jewish students. Students, faculty and staff of many faith traditions participate in the "litany of martyrs" during that week.

Contemporary Art Exhibit

UCM obtained a traveling art exhibit that was designed to generate a "whole mind and body" experience for the viewer. It dealt with the diversity of races, cultures, and religion. Parts of the exhibit were "walk under, step over, crawl through," as well as wall posters. The traveling exhibit was provided through the U.S. National Campus Ministers Association and was used in 1971–72.

International Center

In 1962 UCM opened the first International Center to house foreign students together in a community along with selected American students. For several years CSU was not able or maybe not willing to house such a venture. The UCM and a few faculty members members led by Maurice Albertson rented available fraternity houses, on Shields Street, West Lake Street, then Mathews Street, and finally on College Avenue. The International Student Services at CSU employed a Director of International Student Services who helped the CSU administration see the value of such housing. The UCM-financed housing on College Avenue was closed and is now the Garment District. Eventually the University built a large center on West Elizabeth Street. The Fort Collins community aspect of International Student Services is alive and well and works actively with CSU.

Religion in Life Week

From 1963–66 UCM, the Dean of Students' office, and some of the leaders in the University Religious Directors Association (URDA), organized and conducted a "Religion in Life Week" on campus. Nationally known leaders in religion were invited to address student assemblies, make presentations in classes and lead discussions. These all campus observances were discontinued in 1967.

Graduate Student and Older Learners Luncheon

From 1963–90 free weekly discussions over a soup and salad lunch brought graduate students and older learners together to hear and discuss current issues with CSU faculty members and an occasional person from the Fort Collins community. The "guests" were frequently invited because of their controversial stands, unusual research, or spirituality. They came from all areas of campus life and even included a few administrators. This program has continued off and on in various guises to the present time.

Agape Meals

Beginning in 1964, every Wednesday from 5:30 to 6:45 p.m., students gathered to share an "agape" meal. Students brought all kinds of food to share. The UCM provided most of the beverages. The folding tables were laid flat on the floor and students sat around on the floor. Each meal began with a simple communion ritual. A discussion topic was introduced, food was passed around and some "lively" discussion was common. Some students' only involvement with the UCM was this meal. A woman student from Pueblo proposed the meal idea in 1963. This gathering continued until 1993. A form of this program continues under the title, "Food for Thought."

Senior Students Art Exhibit

In 1966 the Art Department at CSU held a spring Senior Art Exhibit in the Student Center with small cash prizes. Interest was rather low. UCM donated prize money in 1967 to generate more interest. The larger prize money, along with better promotion of the exhibit did the trick. From 1968 to the present, the money for prizes has been a strong incentive and helps makes the exhibit go well.

A Note Regarding the Ongoing Development of Full-time Religious Workers

From 1962–91 more than 50 women and men active in the UCM have gone to theological schools and entered the clergy. These have included: a Roman Catholic priest, two Mennonite ministers, a Jewish rabbi, and clergy in the United Methodist,

Presbyterian (USA), American Baptist, Disciples of Christ, United Church of Christ, and Unitarian churches, and two readers in Christian Science. Several later became full-time counselors or went into social work. This trend continues.

Drug, Alcohol and Youth Programs
Hartshorn Health/Day Service

This very important service for students charged with drug and alcohol abuse is now offered at CSU under the direction of Lisa Miller, a recent director of the Geller Center. It targets students who have a choice of dismissal from the university or entering this rehab program. Over 75 percent have been successful in managing their addiction. **It is the first such program in the United States and has already received national attention in higher education circles.** Teams from several universities have visited and studied the CSU program. It has graduation four times a year. The program enables students to not only stay in school to continue their education, but also helps them to become better prepared to survive in the working world. It is a volunteer program and is not to be confused with punishment. It is a choice between dismissal from CSU and enrolling in the program, and requires a great deal of time and effort. There is a fee for tests in the program that must be paid by students, not their parents.

The UCM — Now and into the Future

A really major change has been that the funding for the ministry no longer is mainly contributed by its denominational connections. Most of the funding comes from individuals, foundations, a small investment fund and special fund-raising events. I think it still is the most relevant and trusted ministry on the CSU campus. The Reverend Peggy Christiansen is the Director/Chaplain and may be the most creative and able chaplain in the history of this ministry.

Our Mission

The mission of the Geller Center for Spiritual Development is to provide a CSU campus and community center that

**nurtures students and
others as whole persons,**

and

**broadens and deepens their
spiritual exploration
and experience.**

The Center is grounded in the teachings of Jesus, honors diversity of belief and practice, works for justice and peace, and cultivates authenticity, integrity and spirit.

A Few Words
about Bob

From Marianne Rieux:

Here you are, Bob

*"When we don't look, we can say nothing
about what happens."*

So . . .
here you are, Bob. Searching
for Schrödinger's cat,
you walk about, wander off
the edge of the world
and
free fall
to the heart of the matter.

Wondering about library lives
you show up
on every body's page,
reminding us — nothing is real
until
you
look.

Time after time, season-
after-season, you search.
In winter,
you cast snow,
clearing a path through
the twinkle.

In spring,
 you
dig about rosebushes and
other thorny things, turning
turning the gathering green:

Life wrecks, crashed cars, babies born,
good byes, good deeds,
good times,
here you are.

Marianne Rieux
Geller Center 'Friday Morning Reading Group'
and Chief, Applications Development
USDA Office of the Chief Information Officer (retired)

From Bobbie and Bill Cook:

Bob Geller has been and will continue to be an important and cherished part of our lives. We met in his Friday 7 a.m. book discussion group many years ago. We continue to participate when we are in town. Over the years we have admired his many community contributions and his initiation of "incubators" to help needed start-up nonprofit organizations that otherwise never would have succeeded.

Bob counseled us when we requested. His sagacity and uncommon wisdom is available to us whenever we ask. He married us, blessed our home, and conducted meaningful wedding ceremonies for our children. We love and respect him more as he and we grow older, and feel fortunate to count him as a friend.

Bill Cook,
Dean Emeritus,
College of Natural Science, CSU
and Bobbie Cook

From Bob Zimdahl:

"When he shall die
Take him and cut him out in little stars,
And he will make the face of heaven so fine
That all the world will be in love with night.
And pay no worship to the garish sun."

William Shakespeare, 1595 Romeo and Juliet, Act 3, Sc. 3

The Reverend Robert A. Geller is Bob to all who know him and that includes many in Fort Collins. Many who he calls friends include those he has helped through life's difficult times, counseled as they considered marriage, and those he has guided through grief. Bob has been an intellectual stimulus, a personal example of how a man should live his life, and a valued member of the Fort Collins community.

Bob has the skill to give his undivided attention to those he is with. They know that their concern becomes his concern and their problems are somehow lessened or, somehow, the problems become more manageable because of time with Bob. Perhaps his finest skill is as a counselor. He is a wise man who shares his knowledge and wisdom with all who spend time with him. That time begins with a conversation, which often becomes a delight, and one departs with some wisdom, perhaps as clarification of one of life's dilemmas. Life goes on, problems diminish, and we tend to forget where the knowledge, the wisdom that led to the solution, came from. It is ours now. On reflection, what we may come to recognize is that was Bob's intent all along. That skill as a counselor and as a friend is one to be treasured. Bob is a man to be loved.

Robert L. Zimdahl
Professor Emeritus
Bioagricultural Sciences and Pest Management
Colorado State University

From the Jean and Bill Griswold:

We first met Bob more than 40 years ago at the Westminster Presbyterian Church, where he and June often worshipped. We felt an almost immediate connection with him: his thoughtful questioning of our assumptions, his international interests, and, of course, United Campus Ministry. Early on he invited me to join his Friday book group. This lasted until the interference of 8 a.m. history classes at CSU forced me to leave the remarkable weekly assemblage of thinkers.

At the church, a change of ministers gave us a chance to experience his pastoral capacity. I later realized that for those few Sundays Bob Geller had pushed us all to focus on change: to keep our theology but change the interpretation, the direction. Sermons challenged us to confront our political actions with our religious beliefs. Bob had a way of preaching by telling a story. Sometimes the stories had obvious meaning, for others one had to think a bit further to get the point. But always they touched on the duty for us Christians to carry out our faith in the lives we lived, comforting the afflicted and afflicting the comfortable.

At the UCM during those years, Bob looked at church-state relations a bit differently from most establishment pastors, not disassociating the Church from the State, but acting within the political structure to effectively change what he and most of us believed was an abominable foreign policy in Vietnam. The UCM became notorious for giving asylum to anti-war protesters. Angry young university students found in Bob, who appeared and looked the epitome of the "establishment," a person whom they could trust, yet who never to my knowledge worked against the laws of the US constitution.

It was during those times that Bob established the bases for several institutions in our city that continue, now on their own, to meet some of our social needs. What would start with citizens meeting to voice an obvious social need in our city would become the nucleus for the growth of an institution helping the poor, helping women in crisis, bringing food and shelter to the needy. Bob acted as the intermediary, pushing here, talking there, always with evident patience to see the task finished successfully.

Personally, Bob has become for us a mentor, a visionary, a living symbol of his commitment to human beings and the faith he follows. He gave personal consolation for Jean's dying mother in his role as pastoral counselor. He was widely known for marriage counseling and presided at hundreds of local weddings. He helped our daughter recommit her vows to her husband at a ceremony in our backyard, an area he knew well for he and June had become "regulars" at the Griswold Sunday Breakfast. For all the professional services he gave, he never kept a dime, but gave the money to the poor and the needy.

One of the most vivid memories we have of Bob's relationship with CSU was the delicate balance he had to maintain when asked to give a blessing at commencement. He knew his audience, its mixed faiths and its celebrating graduates who wished the ceremony were shorter. But he had a point to make, even at the end of a long service. Here it is:

Go in love. Keep your faith. Give your faith away. Work hard. Play enough. Laugh often, and hang loose! So be it. Amen.

William J. Griswold, Professor Emeritus of History,
Colorado State University
Jean S. Griswold. Office of International Services,
Colorado State University (retired)

From Tom Sutherland:

Bob Geller — a true friend and a true gentleman. All the qualities I most admire he exemplifies: a firm but nonjudgmental faith, a spiritual nature, an inquiring mind, intellectual and personal honesty, practicality, a dedication to ministry and caregiving, warmth, a quiet sense of humor...

I've known Bob since our days together on the Westminster Foundation Board in the 1960's. Meetings were held in Boulder, Denver, Fort Collins and other locations around the state which had a Westminster Foundation program on their campuses. We'd drive together to the meetings and talk about everything under the sun, and I grew more and more impressed with his calm demeanor and his knowledge of students and their needs. I could see firsthand how everyone held him in highest esteem. There were hard times and funds became increasingly difficult to raise, but he stuck in through thick and thin, never losing faith and always giving and giving of his time and energy to promote his students' welfare and their spirituality. And those students loved him. It is so fitting that the United Campus Ministry house where he stayed when he first came and where he's given 45 years of service should now be named the Geller Center for Spiritual Development.

He may have officially retired, but he has never truly retired — he gives himself to others for weddings, funerals, unfilled pulpits and special occasions of all kinds. Two of our daughters feel themselves especially blessed by his gift of humor, his soft chuckle, and his love for us with his special benediction: "Go in peace and laugh a lot." And sometimes there is an exhortation: "You can pray all you want, but until you get off your butt and do something about it, it won't happen."

Bob Geller — you won't find a better man.

Tom Sutherland
Professor Emeritus, Colorado State University

From Jim Johnson:

Bob Geller's 85th birthday celebration was a wonderful tribute to a man whom many of us think of as a great man in a true sense. What was remarkable was the wide age range of the attendants. Some were older than Bob (hard to believe, but true), as well as college kids and all ages inbetween. Bob's list of friends extends from the 90's to the teens! Think of that. Most people in their 70's, 80's, and 90's don't have young friends. We know some people who are our own children's ages — but Bob has college kids who like him for what he still is — warm, friendly, caring, curious, alert — trying to stay up-to-date in his reading, and above all, inspirational.

He has counseled people for more than 60 years with unfailing good humor, sympathy, and intelligent advice. He has counseled children about anger management, and teens about handling parents and girl or boy friends; parents about child rearing; youths about career choices; adults about divorce and money management, and seniors about aging gracefully. And he has made friends all along the way.

He was one of the best pulpit preachers I ever heard and I've heard and studied a lot of them.

To me, one of his most endearing traits is his anger — getting and staying angry over our ongoing, never-ending wars with small nations; our prejudice about racial or gender issues, and about stupidity in general which surrounds us all the time.

I shouldn't close without mentioning Bob's comforting presence at a sick bed or at a funeral service.

He is a steadfast friend and I have been grateful for every moment I've spent with him.

His religious beliefs have made him the person he is. Would more of us were like him.

James P. Johnson
attorney-at-law
former member, U.S. Congress

Note:

My sincere thanks to Mark Moody of *North Forty News*, who suggested Bob Geller for the subject in one of a series of articles I did on community volunteers. That was when I first had a chance to write about Bob. Thanks also to Bobbie Cook who wished for a book on Bob's life and made it possible through her generosity. And thanks to Bob Geller who made the last months of 2007 a time of delight for me as I came to know him better and better and to benefit from the sparkle in his eye, the tenderness in his heart, and the extraordinary wisdom in his head. I have never before had work that brought me so much pleasure.

Libby James

Order *Red Ribbons* for a Friend

Telephone orders: 1-970-482-8487
E-mail orders: ucm@lamar.colostate.edu

Postal orders: The Geller Center for Spiritual Development
629 S. Howes St.
Fort Collins, CO   80521

Please send me:

_____ copies of *Red Ribbons* @ $12.50 per copy

Subtotal _____

Sales tax:

Please add 3.7% for products shipped to Colorado addresses

Subtotal _____

Shipping:

US: $3.50 for the first book and $1.50 for each additional book

Subtotal _____

International: Call for prices   _____

TOTAL   _____

Shipping address:

Name: _____

Address: _____

City: _____   State: _____   Zip: _____

Telephone: _____

E-mail: _____